Reviewers' com

Volume I - Pro\[

"What it comes down to is that Blaschke'
different levels - practical, theoretical, (
information in it ... I have a feeling that th
treatment of the subject, could (
- *Kenneth Irving, American Astrology*

Other books in the *Astrology: A Language of Life* series
to order, call 1.800.778.8490 or visit the web site: *www.earthwalkastrology.com*

Volume II - Sabian Aspect Orbs

"What the author has uncovered for us is an underlying energy between any two
degrees in the Zodiac - no matter what planets may be tenanting them. This
precision enables clear distinctions to be drawn between - say - an applying trine
of one degree and a separating trine of one degree (or any other combination of aspect
and orb). And such precision, which before may have appealed more to the
mathematically-minded than the intuitive, is brought out of the abstract realm of
measurement and into the colourful realm of meaning by the inclusion of the
Sabian symbols. What a wonderful world this opens up. Pictures to explain
technical measurements. Right brain married to left. A remarkable achievement,
a fascinating book, and an invaluable reference."
- *Paul F. Newman, The Astrological Journal (UK)*

"Robert has an ingenious mind, with which he examines the Sabian Symbols in a
unique context, that of relating every aspect to a degree meaning. With his usual
thorough and clear explanation, he examines the difference between waxing and
waning aspects together with their applying and separating pattern."
- *Lois M. Rodden, Data News*

Volume III - A Handbook for the Self-Employed Astrologer

"This book is a subtle one. On the surface it is a manual for solid business
techniques, innovative ideas and grass roots common sense. It is so well
constructed that it could be followed step-by-step by anyone starting out in the
profession. A 'no bull' manual for success. Underpinning this is a very emotive
personal story, illustrating the subjectivity of this profession, its anxieties,
emotional content and lack of guarantees. He shows how there is no separating
the person from the business nor the business from the person and does so in a
very ingenious way ... Robert explores and advises on many of the opportunities
that are available to achieve a decent living. There are some excellent chapters
dealing with the logistics of setting up an office, right down to a shopping list of
office supplies, bulk-mailing, telephone services, licensing, marketing techniques,
setting up a school, writing, publishing, lecturing, breaking into the lecture circuit
and associations with other astrologers. He examines the legal aspects of the
profession along with tax liabilities etc. Throughout the book the story of his own
journey from corporate security to soulful insecurity, his anecdotal successes and
failures encourage the reader to learn from his experience, laugh with him and
share his moments of despair. For someone yet to take this journey there is a
heartening message that success can be achieved as he tells us of his journey with
great humility. Robert is totally realistic about the occupational hazards but
never once gives the impression he regrets one moment of his decision to become a
professional astrologer. His writing style is conversational - reading the book is
like having a chat with a well-informed businessman but making a personal
connection with a sensitive human being. He makes it clear that one does not have
to be coy about earning a decent living and does so by spelling out exactly his
own income and expenses ...'*Highly Recommended*' "
- *Linda Reid, FAA Journal (Australia)*

...dedicated to:
all practicing professional astrologers who love and serve their clients...

cover art from a commissioned original oil painting
by Tracy Stinney   October 1998

Pisces 07°
Over the strewn and irregular masses of stone at the shore is low-lying fog, but on one clear rock a cross rests.
[*Lecture~Lessons*; Marc Edmund Jones; 1931]

Astrology
A Language of Life

Volume I - Progressions

Robert P. Blaschke

Edited by Patricia Laferriere

Earthwalk School of Astrology Publishing
Woodside, California USA

First edition published in 1998 by

Earthwalk School of Astrology
PO Box 620679
Woodside CA 94062 USA

1.800.778.8490

www.earthwalkastrology.com

First printing: December 1998 - 500 copies
Second printing: June 1999 - 2000 copies
Third printing: June 2002 - 1000 copies
Fourth printing: June 2004 - 1000 copies

Copyright © 1998 Robert P. Blaschke

All rights reserved. No part of this publication may be reproduced or transmitted in any form or by any means, electronic or mechanical, including photocopy, without permission in writing from Earthwalk School of Astrology. Reviewers may quote brief passages, as may scholars writing astrological journal articles.

Library of Congress Catalog Card Number: 98-94839

International Standard Book Number (ISBN): 0-9668978-0-3

Printed in the United States of America

for my lost daughter, Fíona Giselle
my blood runs in your veins

...the snow prince arrived in the dead of winter
enraptured by one glance from his beloved dancer...
seeing that she was under a spell from a painful past
he drew his sword to slay the dragon
and free her heart...
many battles were fought and lost
and our hero fell grievously wounded
angels came to comfort him...
so in the end a princess was born to the beloved
and for the dragon to be rendered harmless
the prince had to surrender to defeat
and lay down his sword for the quill...

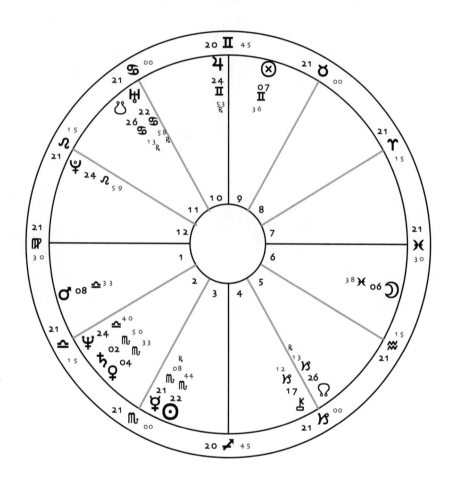

Nativity of the Author

15 November 1953
1:37 AM PST
Santa Monica, California
33N50   118W29
Porphyry Houses
True Node
[from birth certificate]

Table of Contents

Acknowledgments	x
Foreword by Robert Hand	xi
Introduction	1

Chapter One

Astrological Rules, Laws & Definitions . . . 5
    Observation of Transits & Progressions   5
    Carter's Nativity Rule   5
    Carter's Law of Excitation   6
    Leo's Definition of Transits   7
    Then Versus Now   8
    Sensitive Degree Theory - Further Definitions   9
    Endnotes   10

Chapter Two

Progression Theory 11
    Progression Theory - Time   11
    Progression Theory - Metaphysical   12
    Multidimensional Levels of Progressions   13
    Progression Theory - Lifetime   14
    Endnotes   15

Chapter Three

Progressed Planetary Motion 17
    Orbital Motion   17
    Progressed Planetary Returns   18
    Progressed Retrograde Motion   19
    Prolonged Progressed Aspects   19
    Progressed Motion of the Planets Summarized   20
    Progressed Sun Movement   20
    Progressed Moon Movement   20
    Progressed Mercury Movement   21
    Progressed Venus Movement   21
    Progressed Mars Movement   22
    Progressed Jupiter Movement   22
    Progressed Saturn Movement   23
    Progressed Uranus, Neptune & Pluto Movement   23
    Calculating Progressions   23
    Endnotes   24

Chapter Four

The Progressed Sun-Moon Relationship . . . 25
    Progressed Lunation Cycles 25
    Esoteric Definitions of Spirit & Soul 26
    Using the Sabian Symbols with Progressed Lunations 27
    How to Calculate Progressed Lunation Time-Links 30
    Endnotes 32

Chapter Five

Progressed Retrogradation & Stations . . . 33
    Overview of Retrograde Planets 33
    Planets Progressing into Retrograde Motion 34
    Planets Progressing into Direct Motion 41
    Triple Aspects 45
    Progressed Stationary Aspects 48
    Endnotes 49

Chapter Six

Signs, Degrees, Houses & Angles by Progression . . 51
    Progressed Sign Ingresses & Degree Analysis 51
    Progressed Angularity & House Ingresses 56
    The Progressed Horizon & Meridian 59
    Using Decanates & Dwadashâmshas in Progressions 63
    Endnotes 65

Chapter Seven

Discerning Significant Progressed Aspects . . 67
    Preparing for the Client Consultation 67
    Orienting Yourself to the Client's Longer Cycles 67
    Progressed Moon Aspects 68
    Progressed Sun Aspects 68
    Progressed Ascendant & Midheaven Aspects 69
    Progressed Mercury, Venus & Mars Aspects & Retrogradation 70
    Progressed Jupiter & Saturn Aspects & Retrogradation 70
    Transits to Progressed Planets 72
    Progressions Consultation Preparation Checklist 73
    Endnotes 77

Chapter Eight

Miscellaneous Thoughts & Interpretive Strategies . 79
    Synastric Progressions 79
    The Progressed Composite Chart 80
    Progressed Time Twins 81

Converse Progressions	81
The End of Life Chart	82
Metaphysical Time Vector Intersection	83
The Progressed Void-of-Course Moon	83
The Physical Reality	84
The Emotional Reality	85
The Mental Reality	86
Planetary Contact Between Planes of Consciousness	87
The Consultation Preparation "Short List"	88
Final Thoughts	89

Appendix I

Planet Stations 1920-2010 91

Appendix II

Outer Planet Stations 1920-2010 119

Appendix III

Lecture, Class & Workshop Tapes by the Author . . 133

Appendix IV

Astrology Software Programs 134

Appendix V

Computer Chart Services 135

Appendix VI

Contacting the Author	136
To Write the Author	136
Author Availability for Lectures/Workshops	136
Author Availability for Telephone Consultation	136
Bibliography	137
The Sacred Heart of Astrology Correspondence Course .	138

Acknowledgments

I want to give special thanks to my editor, Patty (Chainsaw) Laferriere, who has done a superb job in making me a better writer. It is very difficult to find an individual who is intelligent, literate, knows astrology and is also a writer and editor. Anyone who can deal with my natal retrograde Mercury biquintile Jupiter meandering off into lengthy and redundant sentences and paragraphs is truly a saint. She and I have a composite Mercury-Venus conjunction, at the apex of a Yod, right on the composite Ascendant.

I also want to express my love and thanks to Rob Hand for taking time in the middle of his very busy schedule to read my manuscript and to write the foreword for this book. He sits at a perch atop the tallest tree in the astrological forest, with a view that is incomparable. When he came to Portland last month on the weekend of my 45th birthday, I had the delightful experience of picking him up at the airport and taking him to dinner before his lecture. He is the kind of guy that I would want to drive across country with, talking astrology and metaphysics into the wee hours, with an occasional microbrew and sandwich along the way.

My gratitude also goes to Therese Magee and Charlene Jensen for their editorial assistance early on in the project. To Roy Jones, Betty Steflik and Helena Wolfe, thank you for your technical expertise and help in the cover design. To my friends at *The Mountain Astrologer*—Tem Tarriktar, Kate Sholly, Linda Puffer, Mary Plumb and Judy Schwein—thank you for publishing my articles through the years. I am also indebted to Ray Grasse, TMA's new associate editor, for the excellent job he did in editing my book excerpt article.

Many thanks go to Judith Larson and Anne Lathrop for their prayers, love and encouragement during the time I was writing this book.

To my big brother, Jim, who keeps me laughing like he always did when we were kids, my love and appreciation. To our father, Dr. Alfred C. Blaschke, who sat us down when we were young boys and taught us advanced mathematics; thank you, Dad, for activating my imagination with numbers and patterns, and for passing on your passionate intelligence to me through our family blood.

To Alan Leo and C.E.O. Carter, thank you for whispering in my ear from Heaven while I was writing. I wish you both were still here with us.

And last, but not least, to my elder daughter, Amy Rose, for her heart of gold, tenderness and compassion. I believe in you, my sweet child, and I love you from the bottom of my heart.

Foreword by Robert Hand

In astrology there is one thing that we have enough of, books for beginners. This is understandable because astrology in modern times has always grown through attracting new enthusiasts and it is natural that most texts should be directed at them. However, this has caused one unfortunate condition to come into being. Much of what astrologers actually do is undocumented. We have a good core of written material which is rather basic. But the solid material that actually gives rise to astrology's effectiveness as a practical tool in counseling is passed on mostly by word of mouth from astrologer to student, or in lectures and workshops. The result is that material is lost, sometimes reinvented by another, sometimes not.

This book by Robert Blaschke on progressions is quite accessible to astrological readers of many levels, but it is not a beginner's book. It does not just give the basics of progressions. It goes beyond that to provide a practical and theoretical foundation for integrating the various methods of progression into a single body of method in which each method has its place and there is as little overlap as possible.

The core of the method is based on the three principal forms, common secondary, or day-for-a-year progressions, tertiary, or day-for-a-lunar-cycle progressions, and the so-called minor progressions which are based on a lunar cycle for a year. Conventionally these methods have been used as competing techniques for accomplishing roughly the same thing. The only question has been which is the most effective technique of the three? Whatever the answer might have been, the common practice is to use secondary progressions exclusively because it is the usually taught technique. The Church of Light has also taught that one should use secondaries in conjunction with minors. The minors are used to support the indications of the regular secondaries and possibly improve the timing of events because of the greater movement of the planets within that system. (I believe in fact that the term "minor progression" was coined by the Church of Light.) Tertiaries are the least familiar of the three on this continent, but those who have used them have been impressed with their effectiveness. Tertiaries were devised by the German astrologer E.H. Troinski around the period of the Second World War.

Blaschke's theory is that these three types of progression derive their usefulness from the following relationships. Secondaries are the result of the interaction of the Earth and the Sun (day and year) which in turn correlate to Matter and Spirit. Tertiaries are the result of the interaction of the Earth and the Moon (day and month) which correlate to Matter and Soul. And finally minors are the result of the interaction of the Moon and the Sun (month and year) which correlate to Soul and Spirit.

However, this metaphysical and theoretical framework would be of little use were they not related to practical, applied astrology. While this book is solidly grounded in the author's metaphysical position, it is not an airy, theoretical work devoid of practical application. While pursuing the logic and usefulness of the theoretical position, the book provides much that is useful and practical, and describes techniques of application which may not have occurred to even more advanced astrologers, material on planetary returns in the various systems, cycles that naturally arise out of the various systems and so forth. This is technically a very rich book and one which teaches a definite method which would not be difficult to apply in practice, although some readers may choose to use various parts of the whole system in order to test the overall efficacy of the system. The only warning I would give the reader is that one should make certain that in taking a partial approach to any system, one should be careful not to disrupt the integrity of the entire system in doing so. Sometimes a part of a whole is much less than one might expect with respect to the entire whole.

A question which remains is this: Is the author right, and are his methods for applying progressions the best that there are? At this point I do not feel qualified to give an answer. I do know that my theoretical and metaphysical positions are somewhat different from his. But what I do have to say is that I applaud him for putting the method out whole and entire so that the astrological community can judge it, and that he has done so in book form so that the method cannot be distorted or altered by the more faulty transmission of the word of mouth. Whatever may be my, or anyone else's, final judgment on Blaschke's methods, this book should advance the study of progressions in astrology on both the practical and theoretical level and for this we owe Robert Blaschke a vote of thanks.

Robert Hand
December 1998
Reston, Virginia

Introduction

Welcome to the world of progressions. They are quite possibly the most fascinating and rewarding area of astrological study and practice. It is presumed that you have already studied natal astrology and are seeking to interpret the birthchart as it moves through time.

As the word implies, to progress a horoscope after birth is to move the Sun, Moon and planets in real astronomical motion according to various systems of symbolic, or correlational, time calculations. The birthchart represents the inherent spiritual potential of any human life. The purpose of this book is to define and describe how that life unfolds through time and how individuals *ideally* progress through their lives toward more refined and integrated states of love, experience and wisdom.

This book will also define and describe how reality operates on three different levels and, simultaneously, at three different rates of speed through the mystic time ratio of 1:13:27. The skilled astrologer can use the different systems of progression calculations to identify which plane of consciousness a client is dealing with at any given time. This book will not only explain progression theory but also how to use it with your clients during personal consultations.

In my studies and practice of astrology, esoteric Christianity, eastern mysticism and Theosophy over the past 27 years, I have come to view progressions as an integrative spiritual process and I have a sense of the descent of Spirit into matter that is seen within the progressions. Through my studies and discipleship in eastern mysticism, I have been taught about the mental, emotional and physical bodies that envelop the eternal Spirit. In my studies of Theosophy, I have learned about the upward struggle of the Self-conscious Spirit as it realizes how deeply embedded in matter it has become and begins to feel the painful longing for ascent home. In my experiences as an esoteric Christian, I have seen the flame of Jesus that burns in the universal Sacred Heart and which purifies the perceptions of the mind through intense love and pain in the personal heart.

Progression theory involves the symbolic relationship between the Sun, Moon and Earth. What I perceive is that Spirit, on its downward journey into matter, passes through the minor progressions which correlate with the causal, or mental plane. Planetary impressions are made here in the innermost mind and, in a holographic sense, produce the mental form out of which future emotional or physical reality emerges. These patterns can be found in the minor progressed lunar phases, and in the minor progressed eclipses, stations, retrogradation, aspects, sign changes and house ingresses.

Then these mental impressions make their way downward into the tertiary progressions. The tertiary level correlates with the astral, or emotional/desire plane. Here the impressions enter the feeling body and activate love, desire, anger, fear or dreams. When this occurs, it is directly linked to corresponding previous minor progressed activity, and holographically, has been transported through a time ratio of 27:13.

Lastly, these emotional impressions make their way further downward into the secondary progressions. This level correlates with the physical body. Now the impressions enter the brain, nervous system, blood stream, senses and muscles, and animate the body into either positive life actions, or into illness or disease. When this occurs, it is directly linked to corresponding previous tertiary progressed activity, and has been transported through a time ratio of 13:1.

The flow of consciousness also moves in an upward path, from the secondaries to the tertiaries, and from the tertiaries to the minors. This occurrence is the phenomenon of Spirit in an upward ascent from matter, and informs the astrologer of physical experience impacting feelings or thoughts. When physical or emotional joy or trauma take place, they are transported upwards into the feeling body or mental body. When this occurs, it is directly linked to corresponding future tertiary or minor progressed activity and, holographically, will be transported through a time ratio of either 1:13 or 13:27.

Progression theory suggests that life energy is observable and dateable on three levels of consciousness. Mentally, emotionally and physically we experience planetary influences moving upwards or downwards from one plane to another. The implications are endless. Understanding this, we can link current secondary progressed activity with its previous or future similar tertiary progressed activity. We can even trace it to previous or future similar minor progressed activity. It is my hope that this interpretive framework, which is both metaphysical and practical, will be used, tested and validated by the astrological community at large. It helps us to understand, for example, how memories of childhood abuse can remained buried for years and then, at a particular age, surface. It also helps us to understand how festering thoughts or feelings, unforgiven and unresolved, eventually become chronic illness or disease.

The practical applications of progression theory are almost infinite. It can be used as a diagnostic tool in medical astrology to facilitate healing of chronic illness by linking disease in the body with earlier emotional or mental trauma. In therapeutic astrology, it can identify previous dates and planetary influences in life that are affecting the emotional or psychological well-being of the client. In spiritual astrology, it can provide a metaphysical underpinning that explains how time occurs within a 1:13:27 ratio, and how every present physical experience is directly linked holographically to a previous or future mental impression and feeling state.

I wrote this book with my secondary progressed Sun square to my natal Mars and my progressed Ascendant conjunct my natal Saturn. The book was completed as my secondary progressed Moon left my progressed twelfth house and reached a conjunction with the natal Saturn and the progressed Ascendant in the third degree of Scorpio. The Sabian Symbol for this degree is "A house-raising party in a small village enlists the neighbors' cooperation." I feel that each of my readers is my neighbor in the collective astrological village in which we live. I send this book to you in the spirit of love and community.

I have written this book for the practicing professional astrologer. It is my sincere hope that your knowledge of progression theory and the practical interpretive methods contained herein will allow you to further help your clients. It is my wish that this book will make a small contribution to the existing body of astrological literature on progressions, and, in a loving way, contribute to the spiritual integration of your clients.

Robert P. Blaschke
14 December 1998
Lake Oswego, Oregon

Chapter One
Astrological Rules, Laws & Definitions
Observation of Transits & Progressions

At one point or another in your astrological practice, you have probably observed a seemingly major transit or progression that did not noticeably affect your client. On the other hand, you have probably witnessed a somewhat modest transit or progression trigger major change, pain or disruption. Additionally, you may have wondered why certain transiting or progressed planetary activity operates at one level of conscious experience, but not at another. Also, the question may have arisen as to why planetary activity seems to affect the lives of your clients at different rates of speed.

Through the years, I have also pondered these questions. This chapter is taken from my client experience, my life experience, and the experience of other astrologers. Herein are some basic rules, laws and definitions describing the links between the natal, progressed and transiting horoscopes.

Carter's Nativity Rule

Several years ago, I started to seriously consider the interrelationship between the natal chart and the progressed chart when I first read the prominent British astrologer of earlier this century, Charles E.O. Carter. I found his "Nativity Rule" in *The Principles of Astrology:*

> "It is a cardinal rule that no direction can bring to pass what is not shown in the nativity. Exceptions to this are virtually non-existent."

Carter clarifies a "direction" as the progressed to progressed, or progressed to natal aspects. In essence, he's saying that unless planets are in aspect to each other natally, progressed to progressed aspects or progressed to natal aspect between these same planets will have no significant effect. Exceptions to this are virtually non-existent.

In other words, activity in the progressions that produces life change is derived from the natal horoscope and is only an extension of the existing natal aspects. This means that not all of the potential progressed to natal, or progressed to progressed aspects will equally impact one's life. Carter believed that the natal chart limits the operation of progressions inexorably; the natal chart shows what is likely to happen and the progressions, when.

Carter's Law of Excitation

Pondering the interrelationship between transits and progressions, I found Carter's "Law of Excitation," again in *The Principles of Astrology:*

"If at the time that a progressed body is in aspect to another by direction, either of these bodies forms an aspect by transit with either of the two directional bodies, then this transit will excite the direction into immediate operation."

In other words, when one progressed planet is in aspect to another by progression, and either of these planets form an aspect to the progressed planets by transit, the transiting planet will trigger the progressed aspect. So, within this astrological law, the "exciting" body, or transiting planet, must be one of the two directional (or progressed) bodies. Carter's Law of Excitation works in progressions at every level—secondary, tertiary, and minor and explains why one transit can act with great force while another transit does not.

What the astrologer now discovers is a three-fold link: 1) the natal aspects define and limit significant progressed activity; 2) transits trigger the progressed degrees into manifestation; and 3) at all levels, consider only the same two planets that are in natal aspect.

Comprehending the relationship between transits and progressions leads to an understanding of "sensitive degree" theory: the degrees of current progressed to natal, or progressed to progressed aspects, as they approach exactitude, or just after partile (exact to both the degree and minute), are triggered by one of the same two planets forming a transiting aspect to those degrees.

In practice, the astrologer will find several progressed aspects forming at any given time. Using tight orbs of one degree applying, and one degree separating, a window of time is thus created, showing the overall length of the potential progressed activity. These forming progressed aspects are called *sensitive degrees*.

These "sensitive degrees" are usually part of any major transit to natal, or transit to progressed aspect that produces significant life impact, whether inner or outer. They should always be looked into, along with any transiting conjunctions or oppositions to natal or progressed planets that are not interlinked with progressed sensitive degrees.

In some cases, I have seen another transiting planet, other than the two forming the progressed direction, trigger the sensitive degrees. It is usually the dispositor of the progressed planet's sign—using traditional rulerships: Mars for Scorpio, Saturn for Aquarius and Jupiter for Pisces. A classic example of this type of transit trigger occurred recently on January 21, 1998, at 6:00 AM EST, the morning that the Clinton-Lewinsky scandal broke. President Clinton has his natal Sun (26° Leo 00') semisquare to Venus (11° Libra 07'). By secondary progression, his Venus (26° Scorpio 53') was in a separating square to his natal Sun. Transit Mars at 26° Aquarius 53', *in a partile square to secondary Venus*, triggered the sensitive degrees of the progression. Mars is the dispositor of secondary Venus.

Leo's Definition of Transits

In *The Progressed Horoscope*, Alan Leo officially described transits:

"The word 'transit,' when not qualified in any way, is understood to be the passage of the transiting body over the actual place of the transited body in the horoscope; i.e., it is a conjunction by transit."

What Leo was saying is that the most significant transits are conjunctions. He also stated that the declination (latitude above or below celestial equator) of the planets at the time of the transiting conjunction is also a factor, either weakening or amplifying the effect of the conjunction. This means that a transit conjunction that is also parallel is a more powerful conjunction. A transit opposition that is also contraparallel is a more powerful opposition.

In addition, Leo wrote that transiting aspects, other than the conjunction, to natal planets were of questionable effect with the exception of transiting oppositions to the natal Sun, Moon or Ascendant ruler, or transiting oppositions to the current degree of the progressed Sun or Moon.

Leo also made reference to the existence of "sensitive degrees," writing some 25 to 30 years ahead of C.E.O. Carter, about how existing progressed to natal aspects, during the time the aspect approached exactitude or just after, would be triggered by transits to those degrees. Leo also was quite clear on the point that transits were of lesser importance than progressions.

Leo believed that increased importance should be attached to the transiting conjunctions that take place at the birthday, or progressed birthday, each year. In effect, any conjunction in the Solar Return chart to any natal planet is significant. Also of importance is any transit over (conjunction to) a natal or progressed planet at the time of the year coinciding with the secondary progressed Sun. He felt that these transits would hold their influence over the next year. As did Carter, Leo declared that transiting conjunctions or oppositions to, as well as lunations or eclipses falling on, a current progression's degree points were the triggers that brought the progressed to natal, or progressed to progressed aspect into active manifestation.

The astrologer can make use of Leo's techniques by knowing the current derived dates of the client's secondary, tertiary and minor progressions. For example, my natal Sun is at 22° Scorpio 44'. Currently, my secondary progressed Sun is at 8° Capricorn 28'. This means that I have two birthdays this year: my natal birthday is on November 15th and my secondary progressed birthday is on December 30th (the current derived date of my secondary progressions is December 30, 1953). Any transit conjunctions from my Solar Return chart to my natal chart, or from my progressed Solar Return chart (transits on December 30th) to my natal chart will hold their influence over the next year.

Then Versus Now

British authorities of the early 20th century, such as Alan Leo and Charles Carter, usually using the dates and times of known events such as marriage, death, outbreak of war, accession to the throne, accidents, illness, loss of limb, etc., researched what was happening at the time astrologically by calculating a number of different horoscopes. These charts would include the natal, the transits, at least two or three types of progressed or directed charts, primary directions (moving the MC one degree of right ascension or longitude for each year of life), declinations, and the diurnal chart of the day in question. From this thorough research, they spoke authoritatively about which techniques worked, how the different techniques were linked, and how frequently these techniques were accurate.

As a contrast, the authoritative books of my generation on transits, published in the mid-1970s, seemingly elevated the transits to an interpretive position superior to progressions. As I look back at that era, which was when the first astrological software report programs were being written for mainframe computers, the authors undoubtedly thought that all possible permutations and combinations should be included in order to produce a computer-generated report that detailed all transiting aspects to all natal planets. These "astrological cookbook" approaches to writing, of which the original intention, I assume, was to create an interpretive computer program, have unfortunately served to diminish understanding and discrimination of not only which transits are really important, but also the interrelationship between the natal, progressed and transiting horoscopes.

The reason some transits produce a greater effect, while others do not, according to the earlier British astrological authorities of this century, is in their relationship, or lack thereof, to current progressed to natal, or progressed to progressed aspects. That this astrological rule is commonly overlooked speaks volumes about the fragmentation of good, sound technique brought on by the recent computerization of astrology. In the world of computer programming and usage, as everything is reduced to singular components, the overview, and more importantly, the connection between different astrological calculations, is obscured.

In my experience as a practicing astrologer, the research and observations of Alan Leo and C.E.O. Carter are borne out. Like them, I have found that natal to progressed links, and transit to progressed relationships correlate with the significant life experiences and changes, manifested both inwardly and outwardly.

In defense of transit technique, irrespective of its links to progressions, I have also used the Mars, Jupiter and Saturn transit cycles to their own natal positions extensively and continually find them to be invaluable in my work.

Sensitive Degree Theory - Further Definitions

If you shift your primary reference point of planetary movement after birth from transits to progressions, bearing in mind that all progressed activity itself is directly linked to the birthchart, then the natal aspects become the foundation for all related interpretations. This means that certain planetary relationships, i.e., the pairs of natal planets that are in aspect, will remain prominent throughout the client's life. These planetary pairs are the place of beginning as you establish your interrelated chart analysis.

It is true that there can be significant gaps between the formation of exact secondary progressed to natal aspects, or secondary progressed to secondary progressed aspects, as the day for a year calculations move the Sun, Moon and personal planets at a relatively slow rate of Zodiacal degree movement per year. Taking into consideration the current tertiary and minor progression activity, the planetary picture radically changes. Using a clock of life analogy, with the different rates of motion of the hour, minute and second hands, we find that the secondaries move the planets one day per year (the hour hand), the tertiaries move the planets about thirteen days per year (the minute hand), and the minors move the planets about twenty-seven days per year (the second hand).

This expanded scenario of three different planetary clock hands now creates a steady stream of progressed to natal, and progressed to progressed planetary aspects moving into a one degree applying orb, exactitude and a one degree separating orb. Also, progressed planets enter and exit either the natal or secondary progressed houses. Secondary, tertiary and minor progressed stations—progressed planetary direction reversal—will also result, creating triple aspects and the potential for prolonged aspects to natal or other progressed planets. Progressed planetary direction reversals are always critical and these dates should be carefully calculated and noted. The changing relationship between the three progressed Suns and their corresponding progressed Moons is also highly informative, and the Sabian symbols for the last prior New, Quarter or Full Moons should be noted and explained to your client.

Using this multiple progressed chart analysis as your primary reference, the transits (considering only the transits of the same two planets that are forming a progressed aspect, or the dispositor of the progressed planet's sign) now are relegated to a subordinate role, by acting as the triggering device as they aspect (usually the eighth harmonic aspects: 0°, 45°, 90°, 135°, 180°) the "sensitive degrees" of the progressed to natal, or progressed to progressed aspects.

The progressed to natal, or progressed to progressed aspects are subordinate to the birth horoscope, as only the natal planetary pairs that are in an aspect relationship are considered for qualification for important progressed activity. To summarize: natal aspects are linked to progressed activity which are then linked to transit activity. At all levels, consider only any two planets that are in a natal aspect relationship.

Endnotes

1. Another area of progressions research needing investigation is progressed inferior planet (Mercury or Venus) orbital phase transition, i.e., from inferior conjunction to heliacal rising or from heliacal rising to stationary direct. Progressed superior planets (Mars, Jupiter and Saturn) could also be examined similarly within the scope of this research.

2. It should be noted that C.E.O. Carter, in writing about the Law of Excitation, was not referring to "Solar Arc Directions" (which are a fixed-increment or synthetic movement of the planets, and not to be found in the ephemeris) but to the various systems of progressions which move the planets one day or one lunar month for each year of life in real astronomical motion.

3. A diurnal chart is calculated for the day under review, using the sidereal time of that day and the same time of birth as for the natal chart.

4. Ironically, it was Alan Leo himself who started this "cookbook" trend in astrological interpretation. *The Progressed Horoscope*, first published in 1906 in London, contained outstanding and thorough delineations for all varieties of progressed aspects and sign changes.

5. Birth data for U.S. President Bill Clinton:
    August 19, 1946
    8:51 AM CST
    Hope, Arkansas
    33N40 93W35
    (Source: birth time noted by mother in letter to Shelley Ackerman)

6. Transit Mars was conjunct Jupiter in the 27th degree of Aquarius on 1/21/98.

Chapter Two

Progression Theory

Progression Theory - Time

The systems of birthchart progression are derived from the natural celestial measurements of time: our Earth revolves daily on its polar axis while the Moon appears to orbit monthly around the Earth and, simultaneously, both the Earth and Moon orbit yearly around the Sun. This raises a fundamental theoretical question in astrology: What are the relationships between a day, a month, and a year?

This interrelationship between the different celestial movements is the foundation for the systems of horoscope progression. Secondary progressions—day for a year—reflect the movement of the planets one day for each year of life. Tertiary progressions—day for a month—reflect the movement of the planets one day for each lunar month of life. Minor progressions—month for a year—are the movement of the planets one lunar month for each year of life.

Table 1 - Progressed Planetary Movement

Progression	Actual Movement	Symbolic Time
Secondary	one day	one year of life
Tertiary	one day	one lunar month of life
Minor	one lunar month	one year of life

If the secondaries are calculated as one day of planetary movement per year of life, then what are the relative rates of speed of the tertiaries and minors? Tertiary progressions, which move the planets one day for each lunar month, would then produce ± 13.37 days of planetary movement per year. Minor progressions, which move the planets one lunar month for each year, would then produce ± 27.32 days of planetary movement per year. Thus, an approximate time ratio of 1:13:27 exists between secondary, tertiary and minor progressions. It is my belief that this ratio defines how time operates at three different rates of speed, and how its three-dimensional qualities can be perceived through the three different progression calculation techniques.

Progressions have been likened to the hands of a clock, with the slow-moving secondaries as the hour hand, the medium-speed tertiaries as the minute hand, and the fast-moving minors as the second hand. Alan Leo, in *The Progressed Horoscope*, written almost a hundred years ago, outlined a similar analogy using secondaries, minors and the diurnal chart.

Progression Theory - Metaphysical

No doubt the metaphysician in you has experienced pure intellectual joy in your studies and practice of astrology. One particularly sweet spiritual experience results from reflection on the planetary glyphs and their deeper meanings. Common in the literature on esoteric and theosophical astrology are references to the circle of Spirit, the crescent of Soul, and the cross of Matter. Also mentioned are the physical, emotional and mental bodies that envelop the spiritual self. These three symbols—circle, crescent, and cross—are variously found in each of the planetary glyphs and help the student of astrology to comprehend the essence of the planetary archetypes.

Extending metaphysical correlations to progression time theory, the Sun is represented by the circle of Spirit and correlates to the year; the Moon is represented by the crescent of Soul and correlates to the month; and the Earth is represented by the cross of Matter and correlates to the day.

Table 2 - Metaphysical Correspondences I

Symbol	Spiritual Meaning	Celestial Body	Time Measure
Circle	Spirit	Sun	Year
Crescent	Soul	Moon	Month
Cross	Matter	Earth	Day

Going deeper into the mysteries of the three systems of progression, secondary progressions are the relationship between the Earth and Sun—day for a year. Tertiary progressions are the relationship between the Earth and Moon—day for a month. Minor progressions are the relationship between the Moon and Sun—month for a year.

Table 3 - Metaphysical Correspondences II

Progression	Celestial Relationship	Time Relationship
Secondary	Earth-Sun	Day-Year
Tertiary	Earth-Moon	Day-Month
Minor	Moon-Sun	Month-Year

Journeying further into this theoretical framework, secondary progressions are the relationship between Matter and Spirit (Earth-Sun), tertiary progressions are the relationship between Matter and Soul (Earth-Moon), and minor progressions are the relationship between Soul and Spirit (Moon-Sun).

Table 4 - Metaphysical Correspondences III

Progression	Celestial Relationship	Spiritual Relationship
Secondary	Earth-Sun	Matter-Spirit
Tertiary	Earth-Moon	Matter-Soul
Minor	Moon-Sun	Soul-Spirit

Emerging from the other side of the looking glass, we see that secondary progressions define the experiences of the physical body (Spirit entering Matter—Time Ratio of 1:1); tertiary progressions define the experiences of the emotional/astral body (Soul entering Matter—Time Ratio of 1:13); and minor progressions define the experiences of the mental/causal body (Spirit entering Soul—Time Ratio of 1:27). In this cubic paradigm, we find *reality operating on three different levels and, simultaneously, at three different rates of speed.*

Table 5 - Metaphysical Correspondences IV

Progression	Dimension	Spiritual Relationship	Time Ratio
Secondary	Physical Body	Spirit Enters Matter	1:1
Tertiary	Emotional Body	Soul Enters Matter	1:13
Minor	Mental Body	Spirit Enters Soul	1:27

Multidimensional Levels of Progressions

As an astrologer using this interpretive framework in consultations, you can now calculate clients' secondary, tertiary and minor progressions and articulate the relevant planetary activity affecting their physical, emotional or mental bodies. Through this technique, you can differentiate which planetary activity is moving slowly, at middle speed, or rapidly. What you will find is that thought moves 27 times faster than physical experience and feelings/desires occur 13 times faster.

The five categories of progressed chart interpretation are:

1. Planetary interactions—aspects or movement through houses—between the three progressed charts and the natal chart.
2. Planetary interactions between one progressed chart and another.
3. Any of the three progressed charts viewed individually.
4. Transits to the progressed charts.
5. Transits to the natal chart.

This multiple-chart analysis then creates several categories of planetary activity which must be prioritized down into a "short list" of the most significant dynamics affecting your client. You will find yourself analyzing the following:

(SP = secondary progressed; TP = tertiary progressed;
MP = minor progressed; N = natal; T = transit)

a) MP to N aspects;   b) MP in N houses;   c) MP to SP aspects;
d) MP in SP houses;   e) MP to TP aspects; f) MP to MP aspects;
g) T to MP aspects;   h) TP to natal aspects; i) TP in N houses;
j) TP to SP aspects; k) TP in SP houses;   l) TP to TP aspects;
m) T to TP aspects;   n) SP to N aspects;   o) SP in N houses;
p) SP to SP aspects; q) SP in SP houses;   r) T to SP aspects;
s) T in SP houses   t) T to N aspects;   u) T in N houses

The average practicing astrologer or student of astrology—other than those of you that have Virgo stelliums or retrograde Mercury in Scorpio—would look at these 21 categories and say, "Forget it. Even with my computer astrology software 'hit lists,' it's just too much preparation prior to a consultation."

But, my friend, do not despair. Only certain planetary activity will be considered relevant, and in Chapters 7 and 8, I will discuss how to discern your relevant planetary activity from this maze of all possible aspects and house movement. Besides progressed aspects, the three progressed Sun-Moon phases, eclipses, progressed stations, progressed retrograde movement, and progressed sign and house changes will also be interwoven into our discussion throughout the rest of the book.

Progression Theory - Lifetime

If a natural lifespan consists of about 82 years, then a lifetime of secondary progressions are contained within the first 82 days after birth—day for a year. A lifetime of tertiary progressions are contained within the first three years after birth—day for a month. And a lifetime of minor progressions are contained within a little greater than the first six years after birth—month for a year. At the end of the chapter you can find the calculations supporting this.

Familiarizing yourself with your client's planetary activity in the first three months after birth is essential to grasping the lifetime context of secondary progressions. Additionally, looking ahead in the ephemeris for three to six years for tertiary and minor progressed planetary movement will give retrograde periods, triple progressed aspects, and planetary returns that affect the client in subtle ways. All of this planetary activity, including aspect formation, sign changes, house ingresses, stations, retrograde periods, lunar phase changes, and eclipses is quite remarkably the unfolding of the life force and spiritual growth potential of any individual going through the journey of life.

A lifetime of secondary progressions are the planetary activity contained in the first 82 days after birth, and are the most concentrated seed of life. A lifetime of tertiary progressions occur in the first three years after birth, and are the next most concentrated seed of life. And a lifetime of minor progressions occur in the first six years after birth, and are the least concentrated seed of life.

A skilled astrologer can perceive stressful planetary activity or eclipses forming in the minor progressions which will affect the client on the mental plane. By bringing these to the conscious attention of the client and suggesting positive strategies for integrating them, the energy will not have to move down into the emotional body.

Likewise, a skilled astrologer can perceive stressful planetary activity or eclipses about to form in the tertiary progressions which will affect the client on the emotional plane. By calling these to the conscious attention of the client and suggesting positive strategies for their integration, the energy will not have to move down into the physical body.

If the astrologer finds his client with secondary progressed activity that corresponds to chronic illness in the body, he can research previous stressful minor or tertiary activity to learn the origins of the trouble and help the client in the healing process.

Table 6 - Lifetime Progressions

Progression	Dimension	After Birth	Seed of Life
Secondary	Physical	82 Days	Most Concentrated
Tertiary	Emotional	3 Years	Medium Concentrated
Minor	Mental	6 1/8 Years	Least Concentrated

Endnotes

1. When working with tertiary or minor progressions, a lunar month calculation basis can either be sidereal (27.32 days - 0° Aries to 0° Aries) or synodic (29.53 days - New Moon to New Moon). My client experience in interpreting tertiary or minor progressions has been with sidereal lunar months; I have not had extensive experience researching synodic tertiary or minor progressions.

2. There seems to be no standard within the astrological community for determining the lunar month calculation basis for progressions, although as far back as 1906, when *The Progressed Horoscope* was first published, Alan Leo referred to synodic minor progressions in Appendix I. Amongst the various

astrological software manufacturers, sidereal lunar months seem to be the prevalent calculation, perhaps because the lunar return programming can be extended to calculate the tertiary or minor progressions.

3. If you hypothesize that a natural lifespan would consist of three secondary progressed Moon returns to her natal position, this would equal about 82 years (27.32 years x 3 = 81.96). Thus, a lifetime of secondary progressions are contained within the first 82 days after your birth (day for a year); a lifetime of tertiary progressions are contained within the first three years after your birth (day for a month: each year = 13.369 lunar months; 81.96 years = 1095.72 lunar months; 1095.72 days = three years); and a lifetime of minor progressions are contained within a little greater than the first six years after your birth (month for a year: each lunar month = 27.32 days; 81.96 lunar months x 27.32 days = 2239.15 days, or about 6 1/8 years).

Chapter Three
Progressed Planetary Motion

Orbital Motion

When working with progressions, you will be using correlational time calculations that move the Sun, Moon and planets in real astronomical motion according to the present age of your client. There are many irregularities and peculiarities involved with progressed planetary motion. The progressed planets do not always move through the Zodiac at the same rate because of slowing or accelerating orbital speed as they approach or depart from their stationary points. Also rates of motion are affected by the elliptical nature of their orbits, which causes the planetary motion to either slightly accelerate or slow down compared to the mean, or average rate of orbital speed.

Despite these orbital irregularities, it is still important to familiarize yourself with the average daily motion of the Sun, Moon and planets when working with progressions. This daily motion of the planets represents the standard against which all other orbital conditions are compared. It is also necessary to learn the lengths of the various planetary retrograde periods, as real time retrograde motion is converted into a correlational length of progressed time. In addition, becoming familiar with progressed planetary returns will allow you to analyze progressed life cycles with a greater degree of understanding.

The following table shows the mean, or average, daily motion of the planets, along with the length of their retrograde periods in *real time*.

Table 7 - Planetary Mean Daily Motion & Retrogradation

Planet	Mean Daily Motion	Retrograde Motion
Sun	0° 59' 08"	none
Moon	13° 10' 35"	none
Mercury	1° 23'	20-24 days three times a year
Venus	1° 12'	40-43 days every 1 1/2 years
Mars	0° 31' 27"	58-81 days every 2 years
Jupiter	0° 04' 59"	4 months yearly
Saturn	0° 02' 01"	4 1/2 months yearly
Uranus	0° 00' 42"	± 155 days yearly
Neptune	0° 00' 24"	± 158 days yearly
Pluto	0° 00' 15"	± 160 days yearly

Progressed Planetary Returns

Progressed planetary returns will occur several times during the life of your client. While most astrologers are familiar with the secondary progressed Moon and her 27 1/3 year return cycle, many have not used the tertiary or minor progressions enough to become familiar with their planetary returns.

The following table shows the secondary, tertiary and minor progressed returns—progressed revolution back to conjunction with natal position. Each progression system, each planet within that system, and the length of time are shown. Only the luminaries and planets that have the possibility of completing a progressed cycle within a normal lifespan are considered.

Table 8 - Progressed Planet Returns

Progression	Planet	Length of Cycle
Secondary	Moon	± 27 years, 3.5 months
Tertiary	Sun	± 27 years, 3.8 months
Tertiary	Moon	± 2 years, 13-20 days
Tertiary	Mercury	± 26 years, 9-10 months
Tertiary	Venus (a)	± 22 years, 5-6 months
Tertiary	Venus (b)	± 29 years, 11 months
Tertiary	Mars	± 53 years, 1-2 months
Minor	Sun	± 13 years, 4.4 months
Minor	Moon	1 year
Minor	Mercury	± 13 years, 1-2 months
Minor	Venus (a)	± 10 years, 8-11 months
Minor	Venus (b)	± 14 years, 8-11 months
Minor	Mars	± 26 years, 15 days

a = w/o retrogradation; b = w/ retrogradation

There is an especially synchronous relationship between the *sidereal* secondary Moon and the tertiary Sun. Both take approximately 27 years plus three to four months to return to the natal degree. Also, the 29 and one-half year Saturn transit cycle is closely allied with the length of the *synodic* secondary Moon (progressed New Moon to New Moon).

From Table 8, you will also notice how Venus can complete a tertiary or minor progressed return either with or without having passed through a retrograde period. Normally, the client will alternate between progressed Venus returns that include retrogradation and those that do not.

Progressed Retrograde Motion

It is also helpful to know the length of progressed retrograde periods. A progressed aspect can form three times over many years. The first occurs prior to progressed retrogradation, then again during progressed retrogradation, and lastly after the conclusion of the progressed retrogradation. Obviously, secondary progressed retrograde Mercury or Venus, which move quite slowly within the day for a year calculations, can remain retrograde for many years. Secondary progressed retrograde Mars, Jupiter or Saturn can remain retrograde for an entire lifetime.

It is equally important to know the length of the tertiary and minor progressed retrograde periods as the same kind of triple progressed aspects will also form within these calculations. They will, however, take place over a substantially shorter period of time than the secondaries.

The following table outlines the progressed retrograde periods of all three systems.

Table 9 - Progressed Retrogradation

Progression	Planet	Retrograde Duration
Secondary	Mercury	20 to 24 years
Tertiary	Mercury	18.5 to 21.5 months
Minor	Mercury	9 to 10.6 months
Secondary	Venus	40 to 43 years
Tertiary	Venus	3 to 3.25 years
Minor	Venus	18 to 19 months
Secondary	Mars	60 to 80 years
Tertiary	Mars	4.5 to 5.5 years
Minor	Mars	2.2 to 2.7 years
Secondary	Jupiter	± 122 years
Tertiary	Jupiter	± 9 years
Minor	Jupiter	± 4.5 years
Secondary	Saturn	± 135 years
Tertiary	Saturn	± 10.5 years
Minor	Saturn	± 5.1 years

Prolonged Progressed Aspects

One of the primary reasons to learn about irregularities in progressed planetary motion is to become aware of "prolonged aspects." As a progressing planet approaches a station, stops Zodiacal movement and then slowly accelerates in the reverse direction, it can remain within one degree of its stationary point for days or weeks at a time. In progression calculations, where days are correlated with months or years, these stationary periods of the planets can result in progressed aspects remaining within a one degree applying and separating orb for months or years at a time. A progressed planet reversing direction is significant enough, but a prolonged progressed aspect as a result of a progressed station will just about always result in a very momentous life-changing experience.

Progressed Motion of the Planets Summarized

I will now walk you through the progressed motion of the Sun, Moon and planets. Secondary, tertiary and minor progressed movement per year are detailed, as well as the orbital peculiarities of progressed Mercury, Venus, Mars, Jupiter and Saturn. The outer planets of Uranus, Neptune and Pluto are treated more briefly, as their progressed motion in all three systems is substantially slower, and except for their progressed stations, less significant.

Recalling the clock of life analogy from Chapter One, and remembering that secondary progressions equal one day of planetary movement per year (hour hand), tertiary progressions equal 13.37 days of planetary movement each year (minute hand), and minor progressions equal 27.32 days of planetary movement each year (second hand), we can summarize the planetary motion within each system of progression calculations. *Note that all calculations are based on a sidereal lunar month in lieu of a synodic lunar month.*

Progressed Sun Movement

a) Secondary Progressed Sun: about 1° per year
b) Tertiary Progressed Sun: about 13 1/3° per year
c) Minor Progressed Sun: about 27 1/3° per year
d) Secondary Progressed Sun - lifetime: ± 82°
e) Tertiary Progressed Sun return: every 27 1/3 years
f) Minor Progressed Sun return: every 13 1/3 years

Progressed Moon Movement

a) Secondary Progressed Moon: between 11°48' and 15°14' per year
b) Tertiary Progressed Moon: about 163° to 189° per year
c) Minor Progressed Moon: 360° per year
d) Secondary Progressed Moon return: every 27 1/3 years
e) Tertiary Progressed Moon return: every 2 years and one-half month
f) Minor Progressed Moon return: once a year

Progressed Mercury Movement

a) Fastest daily orbital travel in direct motion: over 2° per day
b) Fastest daily orbital travel in retrograde motion: from 0°37' to 1°21'
c) Zodiac positions when retrograde cause daily degree movement to vary
d) Slowest daily orbital travel at direct or retrograde station: 0°01'
e) For up to 10 days, can be within a degree either side of its stationary point
f) Average daily motion of 1°23' is greatly exceeded during 3-month cycle
g) Fastest secondary progressed direct motion: over 2° per year
h) Fastest tertiary progressed direct motion: over 27° per year
i) Fastest minor progressed direct motion: over 55° per year
j) Potential duration range of progressed Mercury aspects remaining within a one degree applying and separating orb:
- secondary: *anywhere between 11 months and 10 years*
- tertiary: *anywhere between 25 days and 9 months*
- minor: *anywhere between 12 days and 4 1/3 months*

k) Progressed retrograde duration:
- secondary: 20 to 24 years
- tertiary: 1.5 to 1.8 years
- minor: 9 to 10 1/2 months

l) Tertiary Progressed Mercury return: every 26 3/4 years
m) Minor Progressed Mercury return: every 13 1/8 years

Progressed Venus Movement

a) Fastest daily orbital travel in direct motion: up to 1°16' per day
b) Fastest orbital travel in retrograde motion: as low as 0°38' per day
c) Slowest daily orbital travel at direct or retrograde station: 0°00'
d) For up to 17 days, can be within a degree either side of its stationary point
e) Average daily motion of 1°12' is slightly exceeded during 19-month cycle
f) Fastest secondary progressed direct motion: about 1.25° per year
g) Fastest tertiary progressed direct motion: about 17° per year
h) Fastest minor progressed direct motion: about 35° per year
i) Potential duration range of progressed Venus aspects remaining within a one degree applying and separating orb:
- secondary: *anywhere between 19 months and 17 years*
- tertiary: *anywhere between 43 days and 18 months*
- minor: *anywhere between 21 days and 6 1/2 months*

j) Progressed retrograde duration:
- secondary: 40 to 43 years
- tertiary: 3 to 3 1/4 years
- minor: 18 to 19 months

k) Tertiary Progressed Venus return: every 22 1/2 years w/o retrograde
l) Tertiary Progressed Venus return: every 30 years w/ retrograde

m) Minor Progressed Venus return: every 10 3/4 years w/o retrograde
n) Minor Progressed Venus return: every 14 3/4 years w/ retrograde

Progressed Mars Movement

a) Fastest daily orbital travel in direct motion: up to 0°45' per day
b) Fastest orbital travel in retrograde motion: as low as 0°19' per day
c) Slowest daily orbital travel at direct or retrograde station: 0°00'
d) For up to 26 days, can be within a degree either side of its stationary point
e) Average daily motion of 0°31' is greatly exceeded during 2-year cycle
f) Fastest secondary progressed direct motion: 0.75° per year
g) Fastest tertiary progressed direct motion: 10° per year
h) Fastest minor progressed direct motion: 20.5° per year
i) Potential duration range of progressed Mars aspects remaining within a one degree applying and separating orb:
- secondary: *anywhere between 32 months and 26 years*
- tertiary: *anywhere between 73 days and 2 years*
- minor: *anywhere between 36 days and 1 year*

j) Progressed retrograde duration:
- secondary: 58 to 81 years
- tertiary: 4 1/3 to 6 years
- minor: 2 1/8 to 3 years

k) Tertiary Progressed Mars return: every 53 years
l) Minor Progressed Mars return: every 26 years

Progressed Jupiter Movement

a) Fastest daily orbital travel in direct motion: up to 0°14' per day
b) Fastest orbital travel in retrograde motion: as low as 0°08' per day
c) Slowest daily orbital travel at direct or retrograde station: 0°00'
d) For up to 50 days, can be within a degree either side of its stationary point
e) Average daily motion of 0°05' is greatly exceeded during direct motion
f) Fastest secondary progressed direct motion: 0.23° per year
g) Fastest tertiary progressed direct motion: 3.1° per year
h) Fastest minor progressed direct motion: 6.4° per year
i) Potential duration range of progressed Jupiter aspects remaining within a one degree applying and separating orb:
- secondary: *anywhere between 8.6 years and 50 years*
- tertiary: *anywhere between 7.8 months and 3.74 years*
- minor: *anywhere between 3.8 months and 1.83 years*

j) Progressed retrograde duration:
- secondary: ± 122 years
- tertiary: ± 9 years
- minor: ± 4.5 years

Progressed Saturn Movement

a) Fastest daily orbital travel in direct motion: up to 0°08' per day
b) Fastest orbital travel in retrograde motion: as low as 0°05' per day
c) Slowest daily orbital travel at direct or retrograde station: 0°00'
d) For up to 67 days, can be within a degree either side of its stationary point
e) Average daily motion of 0°02' is greatly exceeded during direct motion
f) Fastest secondary progressed direct motion: 0.133° per year
g) Fastest tertiary progressed direct motion: 1.78° per year
h) Fastest minor progressed direct motion: 3.64° per year
i) Potential duration range of progressed Saturn aspects remaining within a one degree applying and separating orb:
- secondary: *anywhere between 15 years and 67 years*
- tertiary: *anywhere between 13.5 months and 5 years*
- minor: *anywhere between 6.6 months and 2.45 years*

j) Progressed retrograde duration:
- secondary: ± 135 years
- tertiary: ± 10.5 years
- minor: ± 5.1 years

Progressed Uranus, Neptune & Pluto Movement

The three outer planets, with their average daily motion of less than one minute (1/60 of a degree), will never exceed 0° 04' per day even at full direct motion orbital speed. Thus, the outer planets progress so slowly as to only be significant when the following occurs:

1. A progressed outer planet stations (direction reversal).
2. A natal aspect with an outer planet progresses to partile.
3. A progressed outer planet having stationed and reversed direction, returns to a partile conjunction with its natal position.

Calculating Progressions

Secondary progressions can be manually calculated quite easily using an ephemeris. There is a formula called the ACD, or adjusted calculation date, that allows you to determine which day of the year for your client matches the line item planetary positions in your ephemeris for as many days after birth as their age. To find the ACD, just follow these four easy steps using your midnight ephemeris:

1. Convert birth time to GMT.
2. Subtract birth GMT from the following midnight.
3. Add this number to the Greenwich sidereal time of birth.
4. Find day of year in ephemeris that matches this adjusted sidereal time.

It is complicated to manually calculate tertiary or minor progressions. Since most contemporary astrologers own computers and astrology software programs, it's rarely done by hand anymore. If you do not own a computer, you can order secondary, tertiary and minor progressed charts and aspect searches from the publisher of this book.

If you are calculating progressions by computer, there is one precaution. You will not know the daily motion of the progressed planets, and thus, the duration of any aspects forming, unless you do one of two things:

1. Refer to your ephemeris for the derived progressed date to determine the orbital speed of the planets and check for recent or upcoming stations.
2. Calculate a dynamic report for a several-year time range that includes the one degree entering and leaving dates, as these will inform you of the total length of time for any aspect influences.

Endnotes

1. You will find computer chart service information in Appendix V.

Chapter Four
The Progressed Sun-Moon Relationship
Progressed Lunation Cycles

As the three progressed Suns and their corresponding progressed Moons move through one's life, the angular relationship between them is in constant flux. There is an approximate orbital ratio of 13:1 between the progressed motion of the Moon and that of the Sun. This means that in all three progression calculations, there will be a measurable synodic lunation cycle from one New Moon to the next.

The following table shows the yearly relationship between the secondary, tertiary and minor progressed solar and lunar motion.

Table 10 - Progressed Sun/Moon Yearly Motion

Progression	Yearly Sun	Yearly Moon
Secondary	± 1°	± 13°10' (varies from 11°48' to 15°14')
Tertiary	± 13 1/3°	± 176° (varies from 163° to 189°)
Minor	± 27 1/3°	360° (annual return)

Because this measurable synodic lunation cycle occurs within the secondary, tertiary and minor progressions simultaneously, one can determine for any period of life the progressed lunar phases of the three Sun/Moon relationships. Each time the progressed Moon reaches an eighth harmonic aspect (conjunction 0° - semisquare 45° - square 90° - sesquiquadrate 135° - opposition 180°) with the progressed Sun, it changes from one lunar phase to the next (New - Crescent - First Quarter - Gibbous - Full - Disseminating - Last Quarter - Balsamic).

The following table shows the length of time of the three progressed lunation cycles and their phases.

Table 11 - Progressed Lunation Cycles

Progression	Cycle Length	Phase Length
Secondary	29 1/2 years	varies from 39 to 50 months
Tertiary	26 1/3 months	varies from 90 to 112 days
Minor	13 months	varies from 43 to 56 days

As you can see from Tables 10 & 11, there is quite an orbital fluctuation with the Moon. As her real-time daily motion ranges from less than 12° to greater than 15°, the length of time for each progressed lunar phase can vary significantly.

Esoteric Definitions of Spirit & Soul

In this complex scenario of secondary, tertiary and minor progressed lunations, there is a fascinating interplay between Spirit and Soul that operates on the three different levels of progressed reality and simultaneously at three different rates of speed. *Spirit* may be defined as the eternal flame of life within, represented by the Sun astrologically. Timeless and unchanging, it has mysteriously descended into matter and longs to ascend back to its home in the heavenly realms. *Soul* may be defined as the mind/emotion matrix filled with its karmic or ancestral patterns, represented by the Moon astrologically. Overflowing with memories, attachments and emotional vulnerabilities, it is constantly changing and lost in time, helpless as it one minute identifies with the divine, and the next minute with the earthly.

In my studies of astrology, esoteric Christianity, eastern mysticism and Theosophy over the last 27 years, I have come to the conclusion that karma and reincarnation theory cannot either be proved or disproved. Therefore, I have adopted a "net result" philosophy towards the natal birthchart factors that represent the "past" and are influencing the client's "present." These chart factors are the Nodes of the Moon, Saturn, Pluto, retrograde planets, the Ascendant and the 12th house. It does not matter to me whether my clients are affected by a past life memory or by the ancestral coding in their DNA which is causing them discomfort, confusion or deep attachment to another human being. What does matter to me is how I can offer them perspective about what they are going through, as the relief of suffering is the goal of life spiritually for me.

Soul, as the intermediary between Spirit and Matter, is the great cosmic stew pot of astrology. The Moon, as the symbolic representation of this dimension of consciousness, is the most active and influential celestial body instigating change in one's life. In metaphysical progression theory, the secondary progressions are the only celestial body correspondence that excludes the Moon.

Secondaries illustrate the Earth-Sun relationship. The implication is that one can potentially overcome karmic or ancestral influences by choosing to act from Spirit that directly enters the body through the personal heart. This is extremely difficult to accomplish and can be viewed as the spiritual ideal of life. It further implies that the heart is a more liberating vehicle than the mind, or, put another way, love is superior to knowledge.

While secondary progressions exclude the Moon in the metaphysical correspondences, both the tertiary and minor progressions involve the Moon in their celestial body relationship. Tertiaries represent the Earth-Moon relationship and inform the astrologer how Soul is directly affecting the physical experience through the emotions and desires. Tertiaries are thus most likely to have an observable direct causation with karma or DNA-related ancestral influences.

The minor progressions represent the Moon-Sun relationship and inform the astrologer of the direct interplay between Soul and Spirit operating on the mental planes (astral or causal). The mystical axiom "as one thinketh, so one becomes" quite literally refers to activity on the mental planes. If this dimension of consciousness is where the law of action and reaction originates, then one can understand the spiritual necessity for purity of thought and purity of heart. This also implies that the minor progressions are the holographic "seed" that either falls on fertile soil or barren ground.

The responsibility of each individual to watch over his own thoughts, following positive visions and restraining negative urges, is an elementary spiritual lesson, but for me, one that I have failed at repeatedly. Yet my higher Self continually encourages me to keep on trying to climb the mountain to get closer to the rarefied air of Spirit. This view suggests that astrologers who understand the current minor progressions of their clients can point out when and how either challenging new thought forms that need to be restrained, or positive visions that need to be followed, are preparing to enter consciousness on the mental planes.

Using the Sabian Symbols with Progressed Lunations

One of the most successful progressed techniques I have used is the explanation of one's current progressed lunation phase using the Sabian Symbol for the specific degree of the progressed Moon aspecting the progressed Sun as it changes phases. The reference that I use is Dane Rudhyar's *An Astrological Mandala: The Cycle of Transformations and Its 360 Symbolic Phases*.

The Sabian Symbols are an esoteric definition, given in pictorial symbolism, of the 360 degrees of the Zodiac. In 1925, at Balboa Park in San Diego, the astrologer Marc Jones and a clairvoyant woman, Elsie Wheeler, collaborated in a venture to use astral means to understand the meaning of each degree of the Zodiac. Additional details of this story can be found in Rudhyar's work as well as in Marc Jones' writings.

The progressed New Moon and the specific degree that it occurs in, describes the meaning of the entire cycle. In secondary progressions, this is extraordinarily important as a client will only experience 2 or 3 of these in a lifetime since the cycle lasts for almost 30 years.

The specific degree at the Full Moon informs the astrologer about what the client has become aware of during the previous 14 to 16 years. At the progressed First and Last Quarter Moons, the specific degrees help clients to understand the nature of their life crises that promote the building of character.

To a lesser extent, I have also referred to the Sabian Symbols for the entries of the progressing Moon into the Crescent, Gibbous, Disseminating and Balsamic phases but have not found them to be as specifically informative as the quarter points of the cycle. Please bear in mind that in Rudhyar's book, the degree symbols are for 1° to 30° rather than 0° to 29°. So, if the progressed New Moon is at 22° 44', you would read the symbol for the 23rd degree. If the progressed Full Moon is at 13° 01', you would read the symbol for the 14th degree. 00° 01' to 01° 00' defines the first degree of any sign and 01° 01' to 02° 00' defines the second degree, etc.

The secondary progressed lunation cycle is a prime tool for understanding how clients arrive at their present experiences. If you carefully research the entire lifetime of secondary lunar phases, you will observe patterns in the New, Quarter and Full Moons. What you will find is that four and, rarely, five successive quarter points (New, First Quarter, Full and Last Quarter) of the secondary lunation cycle fall in cardinal degrees, then the next four fall in fixed degrees, and the final four fall in mutable degrees. Knowing that cardinality equates with taking action and being physical, fixidity with experiencing desire and managing emotions, and mutability with learning and mental development, you can assess the current 30-year life chapter for your clients by correlating their secondary lunation phase with the particular mode and specific degree defining it at the progressed New Moon.

The secondary progressed New Moon rotates through the modes throughout life and informs you which mode is currently predominant in spiritual development.

If you then calculate an entire lifetime of tertiary New, Quarter and Full Moons for your client (quite a list - an 82-year old will have passed through some 37-38 cycles), you will find the same degrees at the beginning of the list that match the secondary lunation degrees. By the age of six, the client will have experienced every tertiary lunation degree that will occur throughout an 82 year lifetime of secondary lunations. This link between the secondaries and tertiaries confirms the facts found in childhood development theory. What children experience emotionally by the age of six will impact them for the remainder of their lives. It is my belief that these are the *"holographic time links"* that inform the astrologer about the connections between childhood emotional experience (tertiaries) and adult physical reality (secondaries). Tertiary New Moons that were also Solar

Eclipses are most likely to have had a significant impact during childhood. To a lesser extent, childhood tertiary Full Moons that were also Lunar Eclipses will also have had a noticeable effect on emotional development.

Each chapter of adult life (lasting from 6 1/2 to 8 1/3 years) as defined by the period of time between secondary progressed New, Quarter or Full Moons, directly corresponds to a childhood chapter of life (6 to 7 1/2 months long), as defined by the corresponding tertiary lunations. The Sabian Symbol for the secondary progressed New, Quarter or Full Moon also has a childhood counterpart in the tertiary lunations that occurred between birth and age six. The astrologer/therapist has a dateable link between present anxiety and/or emotional trauma, and its origins during childhood. Comfort, understanding and healing could be imparted to the client by the astrologer using this progressed time link technique, as the Sabian Symbol for the lunation degree tells the story about what happened long ago that is currently distressing the client.

After the age of six, some additional tertiary lunation degrees will occur that match the degrees found in the lifetime of secondary lunations; some tertiary degrees will occur before in time, and others will come later in time (compared to the lifetime secondary lunations). This informs the astrologer about the law of cause and effect and that the two points in time are distinctly linked. If the tertiary lunations are the emotional experience, and the secondary lunations are the physical experience, then one can perceive a law of causation between them. For example, if a secondary lunation degree occurs prior in time to the identical tertiary lunation degree, then the client is reaping emotionally what they have sown physically (i.e. remorse over inappropriate actions). If the reverse is found where the tertiary lunation degree occurs before the same secondary lunation degree, then the client is reaping physically what has been sown emotionally (i.e., illness brought on by unresolved emotional stress). This technique of progressed time-link analysis has unlimited application for the medical or therapeutic astrologer.

What emerges in a lifetime of minor progressed lunations is that by the age of three, we will have had experienced every minor progressed lunation degree that will occur in a lifetime of secondary progressed lunations. This astrological link to childhood development theory is even more startling as it shows how the mental (minors) development of the child by the age of three will impact the remainder of life (secondaries). Parents can infer from this progressed time-linkage that the infant and toddler needs to be talked to, read to, sung to and engaged in all forms of positive stimulation mentally between birth and age three.

Likewise, each chapter of adult life (6 1/2 to 8 1/3 years) as defined by the period between secondary progressed New, Quarter or Full Moons, is directly connected to the corresponding early childhood chapter of life (3 to 3 3/4 months) as defined by the corresponding minor progressed lunations. The Sabian Symbol for the current secondary progressed New, Quarter or Full Moon also has a childhood counterpart in the minor lunations that occurred between birth and age three. The medical or psychiatric astrologer now has a dateable time link between present mental anxiety and/or emotional depression and its origins because of stimulatory neglect during a specific phase of early childhood.

Similarly, after the age of three some additional minor lunation degrees will occur that match the degrees found in the lifetime of secondary lunations; some minor degrees will occur before in time, and others will come later in time (compared to the lifetime secondary lunations). I believe that this also informs the astrologer about the law of cause and effect since the two points are again distinctly linked. If the minor lunations are the mental experience, and the secondary lunations are the physical experience, then one can see a law of causation between them. For example, if a secondary lunation degree occurs prior in time to the identical minor lunation degree, then the person could experience echoes in his thoughts from what he has done previously. If the reverse is found, where the minor lunation degree occurs before the same secondary lunation degree, then he could be experiencing physical illness due to a previous unresolved shock to his mind, thought patterns or perceptions. This latter scenario illustrates the mind-body connection, and how it can be dated in time.

Since the minor lunations occur just over twice as fast as the tertiaries in the 27:13 ratio, the minor progressed New, Quarter and Full Moons are "preparing the way" for the later tertiary lunations that will occur in precisely the same degrees. This progressed scenario is almost mind-boggling as it intimates how the quality of our emotional life (tertiaries) has a direct link with the content of our thoughts (minors). Understanding this, a person would make a concerted effort to sow thoughts of love, forgiveness and peace, as he would know that he will someday reap the fruits of his mental activity (minors) through his feelings (tertiaries).

How to Calculate Progressed Lunation Time-Links for Your Client

When you are preparing for your progressions consultation with your client, you will need the following chart and dynamic report calculations in advance to evaluate their three progressed Sun-Moon relationships:

1. A bi-wheel chart with the natal chart in the inner wheel, and the secondary progressions for the date of the appointment in the outer wheel.
2. Another bi-wheel chart with the natal chart in the inner wheel, and the current tertiary progressions in the outer wheel.
3. A third bi-wheel chart with the natal chart in the inner wheel, and the

minor progressions in the outer wheel.
4. A dynamic report showing the lifetime of secondary progressed lunations.
5. Another dynamic report showing the lifetime of tertiary progressed lunations.
6. A third dynamic report showing the lifetime of minor progressed lunations.

If you are using Solar Fire™ for Windows, follow these steps to calculate your dynamic reports of the lifetime secondary, tertiary and minor lunations:

1. From the "Dynamic Menu" select "Transits & Progressions"
2. Under "Radix Chart" select your client's natal chart
3. Under "Event Selection" click on "Progs to Progs"
4. Under "Event Selection" click on "Solar & Lunar Eclipses"
5. Remove all other selections under "Event Selection"
6. Under "Point Selection" select "sunmoon"
7. Under "Aspect Selection" select "harm08"
8. Under "Location" select "Natal"
9. Under "Period of Report" use birthday as "Start Date"
10. Under "Period of Report" use "82" and "years" as "Period"
11. Under "Dynamic Type" select "Secondary"
12. Click "Save Selection" as "Lifetime Secondary Lunations"
13. Click "View" to begin calculations
14. Print dynamic report

This dynamic report will show the dates and degrees that the secondary progressed Moon forms a partile (exact to the degree and minute) conjunction, waxing semisquare, waxing square, waxing sesquiquadrate, opposition, waning sesquiquadrate, waning square or waning semisquare aspect to the secondary progressed Sun. These dates are the secondary progressed lunation phase changes (i.e. from New to Crescent to First Quarter, etc.).

Remember that the lunar degree is shown in the second column from the right, and this degree will be the one referred to in the Sabian Symbols. The solar degree is shown in the far right column, and is *not* referred to.

Next, to calculate the tertiary lunations, follow the same steps, except:

11. Under "Dynamic Type" select "Tertiary"
12. Click "Save Selection" as "Lifetime Tertiary Lunations"

Lastly, to calculate the minor lunations, follow the same steps, except:

11. Under "Dynamic Type" select "Minor"
12. Click "Save Selection" as "Lifetime Minor Lunations"

Your printed report for the secondaries should be just one page, for the tertiaries, six pages, and for the minors, eleven pages.

Referring to the secondary report, note the lunar degree and sign of the last secondary lunation shown on the page in the column second from the right. Highlight this degree with a "Brite Liner" and then go to your tertiary report.

In the date column in the middle of page one, find the date corresponding with when your client would have been six years old. This lunation degree should match the last one on the secondary report. Highlight this tertiary degree and date. This informs you when your client had completed a lifetime of secondary lunations in the tertiary calculations. These degrees (the complete secondary list and the first 22 of the tertiary lunations) are the most important time links between the secondary and the tertiary lunations and the most important Sabian Symbols to refer to during the client's lifetime. Any period of the adolescent or adult life identified by the dates between the secondary lunations now has its corresponding childhood chapter shown in the tertiaries.

Next, scan through the remainder of the tertiary lunation list, looking at the lunar degrees in the second column from the right. Search for any secondary lunation degree that shows up after the age of six. The tertiary lunation *must be in the same degree*, not within a degree orb, to be taken into consideration. For example, your client currently is in a secondary progressed Last Quarter phase, occurring in 06° 12' Libra, on September 16, 1996. The identical tertiary lunation corresponding to childhood, occurred on January 28, 1957, at the age of 3 years, 2 months. You may find this same degree showing up in other tertiary lunations during the lifetime after the age of six, either prior to the consultation, or to be occurring later in life. These dates are time-linked and help illuminate the connections between then and now.

You can repeat this procedure with your list of lifetime minor lunations. At the age of three in the minor progressed list, you will find the last secondary lunation degree of the lifetime for your client.

Endnotes

1. To do these calculations, I recommend either the Solar Fire™ astrology software for Windows, or the Io Edition™ astrology software for the Macintosh. Both of these excellent programs are available through the publisher of this book. You will find more information about these programs in Appendix IV.

Chapter Five
Progressed Retrogradation & Stations
Overview of Retrograde Planets

In Chapter Three, I wrote about progressed planetary motion, and included Table 9, showing the length of time of the progressed retrograde periods of Mercury through Saturn in the secondary, tertiary and minor calculations. Progressed retrograde planets, as in the natal chart, are very important in astrology and their progressed stationary points are even more significant still.

This chapter will give you some guidelines for interpreting progressed retrograde planets, as well as provide an analysis of progressed stations and "triple aspects" which happen when a progressed planet forms the same aspect three times over a number of years. Also included in this book, in Appendices I-II, are tables of all planetary stations from 1920 through 2010. From these tables, you will be able to research at what ages your client has, or will, experience progressed stations. They are a handy reference for finding progressed stations as you can zero in on just the planetary information you need to determine stationary degrees and dates.

In my experience, retrograde planets produce alienation, introspection, delay, indirectness, repetition and time-disorientation. Their effect natally is to turn the planetary process subconsciously inward, delaying its outward manifestation and making it more powerful from a self-conscious standpoint but rendering it less effective, at least earlier in life, for worldly interaction and accomplishment.

When natal planets change orbital direction by progression, either from direct to retrograde, or from retrograde to direct, people experience a subtle yet profound shift in their interior selves. Shortly after the progressed station as the planet begins Zodiacal movement, their lives begin to change outwardly, presumably because of the synchronistic relationship between the condition of the inner self and its relation to the world.

The most difficult part of the retrograde experience seems to be the alienation felt from others, or from society in general. Metaphysically, retrograde planets are operating at a different frequency than direct-motion planets and thus, the individual feels out of step with those around him. When planets are retrograde, they are in the portion of their orbit where they are closer to earth, and the influence received from them is much more pronounced.

To get an idea of how common natal planets retrograde are, the following table shows what percentage of the population have the various planets retrograde at birth. The outer planets, in particular, are less important natally retrograde because of their long duration retrograde each year.

Table 12 - Frequency of Planetary Retrogradation at Birth

Planet	Retrograde Duration	% of Population
Venus	40-43 days each 1.5 years	7.7%
Mars	58-81 days every 2 years	9.6%
Mercury	20-24 days thrice a year	18%
Jupiter	4 months yearly	33%
Saturn	4 1/2 months yearly	37.5%
Uranus	± 155 days yearly	42%
Neptune	± 158 days yearly	43%
Pluto	± 160 days yearly	44%

As you can see, Venus and Mars are the planets least likely to be found retrograde at birth. Additionally, they are also the least likely to secondary progress from direct to retrograde because of the length of time of their direct motion periods (greater than a lifetime by secondary progression).

Mercury is found natally retrograde in about a fifth of all birthcharts, whereas Jupiter and Saturn are found retrograde in about a third of all birthcharts. Uranus, Neptune and Pluto are retrograde for over five months a year and, therefore, not individually significant unless closely aspecting the Sun by opposition, quincunx or trine, or near to a station at birth (within one minute of arc of the stationary point).

Planets Progressing into Retrograde Motion

On all three levels of reality, i.e. physical, emotional and mental, and for different lengths of time, we will experience planets progressing into retrograde motion. The secondary, tertiary and minor progressions inform the astrologer on what level of consciousness a client will experience the effect of the progressed retrogradation. Minor progressed retrograde planets primarily affect the thoughts, and, as the precursor to the later occurring tertiaries and secondaries, sow mental seeds for future reaping in life. Tertiary retrograde planets affect the desires and feelings, and, as they manifest subsequently to the minors, are part of a cause and effect dynamic that links previous mental content with present emotional experience. Secondary retrograde planets affect the person through actual, concrete life changes found in the house rulerships and in the physical health. As secondary retrogradation is the final link in the chain of cause and effect, preceded by the tertiaries and minors earlier in life, they're experienced like the caboose at the end of a long train going around a curve—one can see how his entire life so far has brought him to this point. The astrologer, being able to calculate the dates of earlier similar progressed retrogradation in the other systems can inform the client of the time-links between the past and the present.

When a *planet goes retrograde by progression*, the apparent orbital movement of the planet has reversed, and the planet now retreats back through the same degrees of the Zodiac that it has already traversed. This creates two effects:

1. The area of consciousness represented by the planet has undergone a transition from "outer-referencing" to "self-referencing."
2. Earlier experiences in life that occurred while the progressing planet was in direct motion will now be revisited for the sake of review and understanding while the progressing planet moves through those same degrees again.

When *Mercury* progresses into retrograde motion, one undergoes a personal perception shift from outward observance and curiosity about the day-to-day news of the world to more insight, contemplation, absent-mindedness, silence, mental self-referencing or seeming disinterest in the world around them. This chapter of life will last for 20 to 24 years by secondary progression, 18.5 to 21.5 months by tertiary progression, and 9 to 10.6 months by minor progression. It often coincides with a major life-style change as the experience is of needing more time for self than before. As the practical functioning of mind shifts, sometimes clients no longer feel suited for the type of work they have done up until the progressed station.

People born just after a direct Mercury station can live to be 85 to 90 years old and never experience a secondary progressed retrograde Mercury. However, this is more the exception than the rule. Most people experience secondary progressed Mercury retrograde sometime during their lives. Everyone experiences several tertiary and minor progressed retrograde Mercury episodes, with about seven years between tertiary Mercury direct and retrograde stations, and with about 3.5 years between minor Mercury direct and retrograde stations. Someone living to be 82 years old will have experienced nine tertiary retrograde Mercury periods, and 18 minor retrograde ones. These tertiary and minor progressed retrograde Mercury periods should be viewed as times of reflection, reevaluation and rethinking of priorities. Writers or researchers will love these chapters of life and may do some of their best work during theses times. Those with a more gregarious and extroverted verbal nature will be disturbed by them, feeling as if they have somehow lost the ability to communicate with others.

Everyone who experiences Mercury retrograde by progression will certainly be affected by it, particularly in the areas of life shown by the houses with Gemini and Virgo on the cusp. Gemini and Virgo rising individuals are also wholly affected by this progression, and, to a lesser extent, so are Gemini and Virgo Sun individuals.

Parents of children who have Mercury secondary progressing into retrograde motion during the school years will find the child's study habits changing, along with the child developing different interests. The child's relationship with brothers or sisters is also likely to undergo change or disruption. Young people with a secondary progressed retrograde Mercury should be encouraged to develop writing skills, to become avid readers, to take an interest in computers and supported in their desire to be left alone in their rooms. The child may be mistakenly labeled with a learning disorder and parents need a thorough explanation from the astrologer about the nature of the functioning of the mind that occurs with progressed retrograde Mercury.

When *Venus* progresses into retrograde motion, feeling states are altered. I have discussed this occurrence with clients and learned that it is more difficult for them to be emotionally affected by loved ones than before the station and that they are also subjectively more concerned about their own needs. This progression also seems to impact social and financial attitudes, as if the individual has gone through a renunciation of previously-held values about friendships and possessions. This chapter of life will last for 40 to 43 years by secondary progression, 3 to 3.25 years by tertiary progression, and 18 to 19 months by minor progression. Secondary progressed Venus retrograde is an extremely important event, particularly for someone over 45 as it will continue for the remainder of life.

Relational and sexual difficulties are quite common with progressed retrograde Venus and, therefore, the astrologer needs to be sensitive in describing this influence. You do not want to frighten people into thinking that their love lives are doomed for the next 40 years, three years, or one and one-half years, but neither do you want to sugar-coat the complexity of this progression. I have tried to communicate the need to develop artistically now, pursuing literary, musical or creative hobbies and to develop emotional self-reliance so that they do not feel so alienated in their existing relationships. Sexually, especially for women, there may be complications and the suggested remedy would be to advise the client to ask husband, wife or lover to pay more attention to the sensual side of their intimate life.

One could speculate metaphysically about the meaning of progressed retrograde Venus, but this approach would probably not be in the best interest of the client. A more practical discussion would concern the areas of life of the birth chart houses that have Taurus and Libra on the cusps; these are the spheres that will most obviously undergo changes. Trusting that people will eventually receive insight about their changed feelings and perspective in their own ways and at their own paces is preferable to announcing some sort of karmic allegation as to why this is happening to them.

Taurus and Libra rising clients will be most affected by a Venus retrograde progression, yet anyone experiencing it will feel the changes profoundly in their personal life. I have found the Sabian Symbol for the degree of the progressed retrograde station of Venus to be highly meaningful to the client.

Most people will never experience a secondary progressed retrograde Venus during their lives, unless they are born within two or three months before the Venus retrograde station. All people will experience two tertiary and four minor progressed retrograde Venus episodes during a normal lifetime, with about 40 years between tertiary Venus direct and retrograde stations, and with about 20 years between minor Venus direct and retrograde stations. These tertiary and minor progressed retrograde Venus periods should be viewed as times for developing emotional self-reliance with the probability of some painful and difficult relationship experiences to motivate this growth. Artists and musicians will benefit from these chapters of life and may be highly creative during these times. Clients who have a more gregarious and extroverted nature will be disturbed by them, feeling as if they have been somehow socially cut off from the good life.

When *Mars* progresses into retrograde motion, will and vitality are affected. Energy patterns are disrupted by this progression; people will go until they drop without a "heating up" or "cooling down" period. In addition, the competitive instinct now turns inward and, in a sense, the person competes with himself rather than with others to get ahead in life. I have also observed individuals with this progression no longer knowing what they want in life, as if their desires had been wrung out of them like a washcloth. Tragically, in some cases, the date that progressed Mars went retrograde coincides with some act of violence toward the client such as rape, abortion, or a battering, often within a week of the station.

As with Venus, Mars retrograde by progression is very likely to create sexual difficulties, especially for men. At the root, it is not physical intercourse that is the problem, but the desire nature of the individual which is behind the dilemma. The astrologer can attempt to help those who are experiencing less sexual desire as a result of this progression by suggesting that they try to develop the receptive side of their sexuality by becoming more responsive to the partner's needs.

This chapter of life wherein Mars is retrograde will last for 60 to 80 years by secondary progression, 4.5 to 5.5 years by tertiary progression, and 2.2 to 2.7 years by minor progression. When finding secondary progressed Mars retrograde, the astrologer must approach the discussion with positive strategies to integrate the changes to the individual will, sexuality, competitive instincts and desire nature that are taking place.

Aries and Scorpio rising clients will be most affected by Mars retrograde by progression. As they both normally operate from instinct most of the time, usually with fear at the root of their aggressive or self-protective tendencies, this progression will have the effect of turning them in on themselves where their own motives and intentions are plainly seen. A loss of confidence, or its counterpart, exaggerated swagger to conceal feelings of vulnerability, is likely for any client with retrograde Mars by progression. The houses with Aries or Scorpio on the cusp are most noticed by the individual when this progression occurs.

Unless a person is born within two to three months before the Mars retrograde station, he will never experience a secondary progressed retrograde Mars. All clients will experience one or two tertiary, and two or three minor progressed retrograde Mars episodes during a normal lifetime, with about 55 years between tertiary Mars direct and retrograde stations, and with about 27 years between minor Mars direct and retrograde stations. These tertiary and minor progressed retrograde Mars periods should be viewed by the astrologer as times of coming to terms with anger, fear or hurt. The client will feel as if he is confronting himself to accomplish more in life. The astrologer can truly help by discussing the concept of emotional self-mastery during these progressed retrograde Mars periods.

When *Jupiter* progresses into retrograde motion, there is a redefinition of success and its meaning. This progression represents a shift *from* the desire for outer expansion and growth through career achievement, financial prosperity, and community recognition *to* an inner exploration of the spiritual self and a decreased interest in the material trappings of life. I have observed clients with this progression sounding almost embarrassed about their consumer habits and the comfortable lifestyle they had built for themselves. Political and religious views or beliefs will undergo a transition and old friends may no longer be relevant to one's new vision of life. The client may need to talk about a crisis in faith at the time of this progressed station, as previously held beliefs based on the family religion, or on the influence of others, no longer are meaningful to them.

Sagittarius and Pisces rising clients will feel as if their lives have been turned upside down with Jupiter progressing into retrograde motion, and, to a lesser extent, so will Sagittarius and Pisces Sun individuals. In all cases, the houses with these signs on the cusp will be most affected by this progression. This chapter of life will last for over 120 years by secondary progression, and thus, for the remainder of life. Tertiary progressed Jupiter will remain retrograde for about nine years, and minor progressed Jupiter for about 4.5 years. The influence of secondary progressed retrograde Jupiter may take a few years after the station to be felt consciously by the client, as stationary Jupiter remains in the same degree and minute for three to seven days in real time, and thus, three to seven years in secondary time.

As Jupiter remains in direct motion for eight months in real time, one will never experience a secondary progressed retrograde Jupiter, unless born within two to three months of the retrograde station. However, everyone will experience two or three tertiary and five or six minor progressed retrograde Jupiter episodes during a normal lifetime, with about 21 years between tertiary Jupiter direct and retrograde stations, and with about 10 years between minor Jupiter direct and retrograde stations. These tertiary and minor progressed retrograde Jupiter periods should be viewed as times of either dissatisfaction with success because of misalignment between spiritual and worldly values, or as periods where one consciously chooses to forego career growth to pursue the inner life more richly. In either case, clients will, ideally, define for themselves the meaning of personal success and satisfaction during these Jupiter retrograde periods.

When *Saturn* progresses into retrograde motion, there are changes in how one relates to authority. Instead of the social status quo defining goals and ambitions, one shifts to an inner definition of character, achievement and purpose. This progression often coincides with a disorienting career change for people as they no longer feel able to take direction or supervision from bosses or employers as before. The astrologer would be wise to discuss self-employment with a client during this progressed station, as being one's own boss would be in keeping with the nature of retrograde Saturn. As with retrograde Jupiter, clients may also find themselves questioning the meaning of success. Retrograde Saturn, however, has more to do with feelings of inadequacy or defeat from not having achieved goals or ambitions. Often, though, these goals or ambitions weren't from the heart's intention but from other's expectations.

Capricorn and Aquarius rising individuals will be most affected by Saturn progressing into retrograde motion as it will affect their entire outlook on life. Those with a Capricorn or Aquarius Sun will also be highly affected by this progression, becoming more and more aware of the inner origins of their principles and morals. All people with this progression, however, will have to be on guard against mental depression as retrograde Saturn tends to make a person extremely self-critical. The houses with Capricorn and Aquarius on the cusps will show the areas of life most affected by this progression. This chapter will last for the rest of life by secondary progression, for about 10.5 years by tertiary progression, and for about five years by minor progression. In discussing the secondary progressed retrograde station of Saturn with the client, the astrologer needs to present the meaning of it as a constant and enduring change. The influence of secondary progressed retrograde Saturn may take a few years after the station to be felt consciously by the client, as stationary Saturn remains in the same degree and minute for three to eight days in real time, and thus, three to eight years in secondary time.

Unless born within two to three months of the retrograde station, one will never experience a secondary progressed retrograde Saturn. Everyone will experience two or three tertiary and five or six minor progressed retrograde Saturn episodes during a normal lifetime, with about 18 years between tertiary Saturn direct and retrograde stations, and with about eight and two-thirds years between minor Saturn direct and retrograde stations. These tertiary and minor progressed retrograde Saturn periods are times of reviewing life goals and/or periods of hard work and effort that will bear fruit later in life. There may also be health complications during these retrograde Saturn periods, particularly, if rigidly holding onto self-protective armor over the heart and ego defenses that mask vulnerability. There is nothing quite as effective as sickness and/or chronic illness to drop people to their knees (Saturn) for the sake of spiritual surrender.

I do not attach much significance to Uranus, Neptune or Pluto's progressions into retrograde motion, unless the client has a close (less than 2° orb) natal aspect to the Sun by these planets, or unless the client was born on or near an outer planet station (within one minute of arc). In these cases, progressed stationary retrograde Uranus would result in a withdrawal inward of non-conformist urges. Potentially, one could decide to get a "straight" job to appear to fit in like everybody else, while keeping the "inner rebel" intact.

Progressed stationary retrograde Neptune would either coincide with a personal spiritual awakening where clients have the lid blown off their world views, or a lapse into addictive behaviors to cope with the confusion or chaos they feel within. Artists and musicians, especially, could use the retrograde Neptune frequency to be highly productive.

Progressed stationary retrograde Pluto would result in more privacy and secrecy. With it, one would be capable of transforming personal emotional turmoil into inner spiritual power. The client would probably have to deal with obsessive and compulsive thoughts or feelings after the station, until he gets a handle on why these primitive survival instincts keep surfacing as if he were involved in some kind of life-threatening situation.

Because the stationing outer planets remain in the same degree and minute for seven to 16 days in real time, by secondary progression one will not receive any retrograde motion by these planets for four to eight years after the station. It is only in looking back on life from about 20 years down the road that people can identify with their secondary progressed outer planets having gone retrograde. However, tertiary and minor progressed Uranus, Neptune and Pluto will be retrograde several times during life, and these faster progression calculations get the outer planets moving again soon after the station. With all the progressed activity going on at any given time for the client, I, personally, would rather spend consultation time discussing just the effects of progressed Mercury through Saturn.

Planets Progressing into Direct Motion

When a *planet goes direct by progression*, an exteriorization of the life force takes place. Additionally, there is a relaxing of the extreme subjectivity associated with that area of consciousness defined by the retrograde planet. Feelings of social, intellectual or spiritual alienation can lift around the direct station. The client may now feel ready to show up for life and work toward personal accomplishment. The direct station of a planet has been classically described as a process of emergence occurring after a period of internal shaping. At these stations, clients describe feelings of release from some vague sense of karmic retribution. They sense the possibility of going forward into the fulfillment of lifelong hopes.

When you ponder the significance of the secondary progressed direct station of a planet retrograde since birth, what comes to mind is that the client has never known what it is to experience this planet in a "normal" way. There is usually excitement, anticipation and joy around the time of the progressed direct station. The client needs encouragement to believe in himself, to know deeply in his heart that the creative contribution he can make in life is very worthwhile.

With all progressed planet direct stations, the astrologer should bring up for discussion the houses ruled by the planet going direct by progression. I recommend using the traditional house cusp rulerships of Mercury for Gemini and Virgo, Venus for Taurus and Libra, Mars for Aries and Scorpio, Jupiter for Sagittarius and Pisces, Saturn for Capricorn and Aquarius. These houses will be activated by the direct station through the planetary ruler, and, in the case of angular houses, can alter the structure of life altogether.

Natal retrograde *Mercury* secondary progressing into direct motion, occurring no later than the age of 24, is of special interest to parents. Your silent and shy child may now find himself becoming popular, well-liked and admired for conversational abilities. Before the direct station, the young person may have stuttered, felt less intelligent than classmates, or too shy to assert himself. Now it is as if his mind has been retooled. Tracy Marks, in *The Art of Chart Interpretation,* made the astute observation that retrograde planets represented *energies one was not encouraged to express outwardly during childhood,* and, therefore, must be developed by the individuals themselves.

One of the best examples of this concept regarding retrograde planets, besides my own personal experience, was from the glib, Gemini football star, Joe Namath, on a televised "celebrity roast." He said that he thought his name was "Shut Up" until he was five years old. Sure enough, he has natal retrograde Mercury at 27° Taurus. It progressed to direct motion between the age of four and five.

My personal example of natal retrograde Mercury supports this concept of unencouraged behavior. At the dinner table, my father told me repeatedly to "be quiet" so that he could listen to my older brother speak first about his day at school. I also stuttered as a young boy and was beset by feelings of unworthiness that had to be worked through before writing this book. However, when individuals have to develop parts of themselves without parental encouragement, determination to succeed reaches quite deep.

When you have a client with a natal retrograde Mercury which went direct by progression during youth, it is very helpful to determine the age this occurred and discuss it with the client. Generally, it's the time of an important turning point. It is also therapeutic to discuss the absence of encouragement for mental and communicative skills and to compliment the ability to articulate that has been developed.

A special consideration must be given to a natal direct motion Mercury that previously progressed into retrograde motion, and is now progressing back into direct motion. The client may experience the feeling of having been mentally "off track" for 20 to 24 years by secondary progression, for about 20 months by tertiary progression, and for about 10 months by minor progression. When finished, he is ready to resume the life direction to which he had previously aspired. The astrologer should research the date and degree of the retrograde station and compare it to the direct station. These dates can then be presented to the client in a "bookends" metaphor, helping to explain the long-term perspective of why and when he has twice undergone a perceptual transformation.

The most significant progression of *Venus* into direct motion is when the client has this planet natally retrograde and experiences the secondary progressed direct station, always before the age of 43. If the client is in his 30s or early 40s when this occurs, there is likely to be a history of sexual and relationship problems and the astrologer needs to plunge into this territory with care and sensitivity during the consultation.

Clients with natal retrograde Venus describe themselves as "broken," as if they had reached the conclusion that they were failures in relationships and that they had given up on love. There is a resurrection of the heart that happens at the direct station of Venus and the client needs the assurance that it is better to risk love again and live in a state of redemption than to exist having surrendered to defeat in relationships.

The direct station of secondary progressed Venus, when not retrograde at birth, can only occur past the age of 44. Here the client, usually in his 50's or 60's, has spent over 40 years with this retrograde progression and is now experiencing an emergence of the heart. It is wise to determine the date and degree of the retrograde station and discuss the Sabian symbols for both the direct and retrograde stationary degrees.

Most clients will experience two tertiary progressed and four minor progressed direct stations of Venus during their lifetimes. At the tertiary stations, which follow a three-year retrograde episode, the client experiences an emotional time-link connected to an earlier chapter in life. The astrologer should research when the identical minor progressed direct station of Venus occurred in precisely the same degree, which followed a one and one-half year retrograde period, and bring this minor stationary date up for discussion in connection with the tertiary stationary date. These periods in life can be anywhere from ten to 40 years apart. There is a direct cause and effect relationship between the preceding minor progressed station and the succeeding tertiary progressed station. The Sabian symbol for this degree is highly informative.

When *Mars* progresses into direct motion, one can now act on a powerful inner reservoir of energy that has been building for the length of the preceding retrograde period. The progressed direct station of Mars is a crucial turning point in life, for now the client can go after what he really wants with the will power and drive to make it happen. Secondary progressed Mars direct after a lifetime of retrogradation can occur at any time in the client's life up to between the ages of 60-80. The fact that the client *is* experiencing this progression suggests that there is something within that is dying to come out and be expressed.

Mars, in my opinion, is most underrated as a creative planet. The astrologer can genuinely help the client with a progressed direct station of Mars by asking point-blank, "What do you want?" It's a spiritual axiom that unless people know exactly what they desire, they can never obtain it. The astrologer would be wise to remind the client of this.

Most clients will experience one or two tertiary, and two or three minor progressed direct stations of Mars during their lives. At the tertiary station, which follows a five-year retrograde period, the client will be experiencing the exact same degree of stationary Mars that occurred earlier in life at the minor progressed station, which followed a two and one-half year retrograde period. These two dates, which may be from 10 to 40 years apart, will inform the astrologer of a time link in the client's life. The Sabian symbol for this degree is very important as it describes how the individual will must harmonize with Divine Will.

Jupiter progressing into direct motion discloses the hidden meaning of the client's next phase of spiritual growth. The Sabian symbol for the stationary direct degrees of Jupiter by secondary, tertiary or minor progression can be so revealing to the client as to provoke sighs of relief and tears of deep understanding.

Jupiter, as ruler of Pisces, represents spiritual synthesis, and thus, the power to integrate the concealed and deeper universal sympathies and emotions that are necessary for further spiritual growth. Jupiter also rules the arterial blood and this metaphor informs the astrologer of how the love hidden deep in the heart is spread throughout the body, animating it and giving it life. The direct stations of Jupiter speak to this process.

As Jupiter remains retrograde for four months in real time each year, which translates into over 120 years in secondary progressed time, clients with natal retrograde Jupiter will never experience it direct by secondary progression unless they are born within two to three months before the direct station. However, all clients will experience two or three tertiary, and five or six minor progressed direct Jupiter stations during life, which follow either a nine-year tertiary retrograde period, or a four and one-half year minor retrograde period. The astrologer can be of incalculable service to the client spiritually by researching and discussing the degrees and dates of the retrograde and direct stations of Jupiter using the Sabian symbols to tell the story. The astrologer can also inform the client about the "time-links" between the previously occurring minor progressed direct stations and their later-in-life counterparts falling in the identical degrees—the tertiary progressed direct stations. The client can gain valuable spiritual perspective through this.

Saturn progressing into direct motion reveals how and when one reaps what has been sown in life. The progressed stations of Saturn are the pivotal points in life where the client has the opportunity to *either* learn deeply from experience, integrating it into a more mature and wiser consciousness, *or* instead to build more armor and defenses around the truth contained in the heart, which then leads to a continuation of the false self and eventual chronic illness and/or disease.

Esoterically, Saturn, ruler of the knees, the bones, and atonement brings one to his knees in spiritual submission and repentance for mistakes. Failing submission and repentance, one's very bones are compromised affecting physical health. When this atonement is accomplished spiritually, Jupiter, which rules bone marrow, then activates and restores the spirit force in the body by producing new and healthy bone marrow.

As Saturn stays retrograde for four and one-half months in real time each year, clients with natal retrograde Saturn will never experience a direct Saturn by secondary progression unless they are born within two to three months of the direct station. All people will experience three tertiary and five or six minor progressed direct Saturn stations in a normal lifetime. These follow either a ten and one-half year tertiary retrograde period, or a five year minor progressed retrograde period. The tertiary direct stations of Saturn fall in the same degrees as the preceding minor progressed direct stations, showing the astrologer the progressed time-link connecting different chapters of the client's life. The dates of these direct and retrograde stations, along with the Sabian symbols for the stationary degrees, should be researched and presented to illustrate the specific lessons of experience that are necessary to spiritual integration and physical health.

As mentioned earlier, I do not find much significance in Uranus, Neptune or Pluto's progressions into direct motion unless the client has a close natal aspect to the Sun by these planets (less than 2° orb), or unless the client was born on or near an outer planet station (within 1' of arc). As discussed previously, the outer planets remain stationary in the same degree and minute for seven to 16 days in real time, and thus, by secondary progression for seven to 16 years. Therefore, it takes several years for the planet to begin secondary progressed orbital movement after stationing. These secondary progressed outer planet direction reversals are usually only understood by looking back on life 20-30 years later.

The tertiary and minor progressed direct stations of Uranus, Neptune or Pluto can be researched if the client has a close natal aspect to the Sun from one of these planets, or if they were born at a station. As mentioned before, I would pay more attention to progressed Mercury through Saturn, not to mention the progressed Sun and Moon, during the limited time of the consultation. By doing your homework on progressed Sun through Saturn properly prior to a consultation, you will always be able to discuss progressed planetary influences which speak to the very heart and soul of your client.

Triple Aspects

Because of progressed retrogradation, the same aspect from a progressed planet to a natal planet may form three times over many years with two stations occurring between the three aspects. This experience is akin to "triple transits," where the transiting planet forms three, or in the cases of Neptune or Pluto, sometimes five exact aspects to the natal planet. However, in progression calculations, the duration of these aspects from the progressed to the natal planet is much longer and, hence, they represent long-term life lessons and more gradual processes.

The softwood-hardwood metaphor explains the meaning of triple aspects: one blow of the hammer will drive a nail into softwood yet three, or even five blows, may be necessary to drive the nail into hardwood. Human consciousness has equal parts receptivity (Jupiter) and resistance (Saturn) towards growth and spiritual integration, so the esoteric astrologer can readily understand why clients require several planetary "blows" to reach a place of spiritual understanding.

Since multiple transit aspects occur within a relatively short period of time, some clients wind up just persevering through the entire transit episode without truly having been changed by it because of the condensed time period in which it occurred.

Because progressed triple aspects occur over such a long period, the astrologer can use these progressed dates as mileposts in facilitating long-term understanding of the spiritual meaning of the events brought on by these transits. Progressions are a primary tool for a lifetime perspective.

Most people, when under the influence of hard, multiple transits from Saturn, Uranus, Neptune or Pluto, lasting between 10-20 months, *have no idea what it all means until some time has passed*. No one can know with any certainty *what the eventual lessons and outcomes of these transits will be*. But clients can be helped by researching current progressed activity and how it is linked in time to earlier identical progressed lunations, stations or aspects. These are lessons revisited and they can provide a broader perspective about the life changes one is undergoing.

To familiarize yourself with these techniques, start by calculating an entire lifetime of 82 years of the tertiary and minor progressions of Mars, Jupiter and Saturn. Limit the aspect selection to conjunction and opposition only. Doing this, you will find four to six tertiary stations and six to 12 minor progressed stations of these planets. Pay particular attention to the retrograde degree spans of Mars (about 10-16°), Jupiter (about 10°) and Saturn (about 6-7°) by progression, as you can see from these degree spans if any aspects formed to natal planets. If yes, then there will also be two other identical aspects forming to the same natal planet, one before the retrograde period, and one after it. For example, if tertiary progressed direct Jupiter is conjunct natal Uranus in January of 1976, then tertiary Jupiter stations retrograde in April of 1981. Next, tertiary Jupiter makes a retrograde conjunction to natal Uranus in November of 1986, then tertiary Jupiter stations direct in April of 1990. Finally, tertiary Jupiter forms the third and last conjunction to natal Uranus in September 1993.

As you can see from this example, the entire episode lasted for 17 and one-half years from the first progressed conjunction to the third one. In between, two stations occurred, one retrograde and one direct, about four to five years apart from the aspects being formed. Determine the stationary degrees of progressed Jupiter, refer to the Sabian symbols for them, and present this entire scenario to the client in a cohesive, long-term perspective.

Knowing that Jupiter-Uranus progressed aspects will speak to the client's spiritual breakthroughs, and knowing that tertiary progressions operate on the emotional plane, you can then weave a complete story about what this all means for your client and present it to him for discussion. This technique refers to dates in life already passed, but it also can be used when the client is still in the middle of the five-part scenario, say, between the retrograde conjunction and the direct station. With this timeline, you can help the client by explaining when the episode began, how far into it he is and how much longer it will continue. The benefit to the client is in the gradual, long range perspective which can be more readily integrated and understood compared to time-dense transits.

In secondary progressions, triple aspects can occur over several decades and can literally define a significant portion of the overall life-purpose. Recently, "Marie," age 61, came in to see me for a progressions consultation. She had just completed negotiations for teaching a series of classes on spiritual development at a local university. This teaching position meant the fulfillment of a life-long ambition she had dreamed about since her teenage years.

Marie's natal Mercury was at 27° Leo, and her natal Neptune at 18° Virgo. At the age of 15, secondary progressed Mercury formed a conjunction to her natal Neptune. This was when she had originally conceived the idea to teach spirituality. Then, at age 33, secondary progressed Mercury went stationary retrograde at 30° Virgo. She had the retrograde conjunction of progressed Mercury to natal Neptune at age 51. Secondary Mercury went stationary direct at age 56 at 16° Virgo. Finally, when I saw her, progressed Mercury was forming the third and final conjunction to natal Neptune at age 61. This triple aspect episode was now concluding 46 years of personal endeavor for her, and I shared in her joy of fulfilling her lifetime aspiration.

For a long time, during the progressed retrograde Mercury period lasting 23 years, Marie said she had felt far removed from her original vision. But now she saw how she was being shaped and prepared from within during that time. At age 56, when the direct station occurred, she began to emerge and teach small groups. Now, at last securing a prestigious teaching position at a university confirmed and validated her spiritual qualities and knowledge. Marie's story illustrates the strength of personal vision that traverses years and years.

The career consulting astrologer develops personal relationships with clients over the years and is privy to the most intimate hopes and dreams that they carry in their hearts. Through thorough research of your clients lifetime of progressed activity, you will be able to perceive the story lines that run through their overall life scripts. Knowing these progressed story lines, such as triple aspects, the degrees of their progressed stations, and where they are in their progressed lunation cycle, puts the astrologer in a rare position to give encouragement, guidance and direction when clients need help and service.

Progressed Stationary Aspects

Chapter Three included discussion of the progressed motion of the Sun, Moon and planets. The sections for the progressed planetary movement includes information about the potential duration range of progressed Mercury through Saturn forming aspects with a natal planet within a one degree applying and separating orb. This shows how long it takes a progressed planet to move in and out of an aspect with a natal planet at full orbital motion. It also shows the duration of an aspect when the progressed planet stations and remains within a one degree orb of aspecting a natal planet for many years.

In the case of secondary progressed Mercury, for example, which can move over 2° per year at full orbital motion, an aspect with a natal planet can come and go within an 11 month window—one degree applying, partile aspect, one degree separating. However, when Mercury approaches a progressed station, it can remain within one degree of the stationary point for 10 years. If, while progressed Mercury approaches a direct or retrograde station, it also is forming an aspect to a natal planet, the duration of influence of this progressed aspect can be eleven times as long as the aspect being formed at full orbital motion.

In my practice, I have seen many clients who had a secondary progressed Mercury stationing while holding a conjunction, square, quincunx or opposition to natal Saturn or Neptune. Many of them were on medication for clinical depression during the time of the prolonged aspect (ten years). After the station, when progressed Mercury began to move again and leave the one degree separating orb, the clients would report that the depression had lifted, and that they were able to discontinue medication. While the astrologer cannot neutralize the effect of a stressful prolonged progressed aspect such as this, he can comfort the client by informing him how long it will last, and how he may employ positive strategies to offset its negative effects.

Several clients born in late 1949 had secondary progressed Venus go stationary retrograde at 18° Aquarius while holding an opposition within a 1° orb to natal Pluto for over 17 years. Their stories of relationship endings and pain spread out over such a long chapter of their lives were heartbreaking but at least I could provide a time perspective and other comforting news by advising them when it would lift.

Other clients born in January 1935 had secondary progressed Mars go stationary retrograde at 24° Libra while holding a square within a 1° orb to natal Pluto for over 26 years. Talk about transforming the will in this lifetime.

The tables in Appendices I and II provide all planetary stations occurring between 1920 and 2010. Find the table for the year of your client's birth and then proceed to look at the three months after the birthday. Make notes about any direct or retrograde stations you find, listing the degree and how many days after the birthday they occur. This will inform you at what age the client has, or will, experience these secondary progressed stations.

Next, look at their natal chart and see if the degree of the planetary station was within a 1° orb of forming a conjunction, opposition, trine, square, sextile, semisquare, sesquiquadrate or quincunx to a natal planet, lunar node, ascendant or midheaven. If yes, then you will have found a prolonged progressed aspect. Stationary secondary Mercury aspects can last up to 10 years, Venus for 17 years, Mars for 26 years, Jupiter for 50 years, and Saturn for 67 years.

The tables in Appendices I and II can also be used to locate tertiary and minor progressed stations but it is more difficult to "eyeball" the age of the client when these would occur than with the secondaries. As you remember, a lifetime of 82 years of tertiary progressions will occur within the first three years after birth. Therefore, at age 41, a client will have a derived tertiary progressed date of about 18 months after birth. As a lifetime of minor progressions occur within the first six and one-eighth years after birth, a 40- year-old client will have a derived minor progressed date of about 3 years after birth. Meticulous and thorough astrologers will want to scan these tables for the six years after birth and make notes of any stationary degrees that would form conjunctions, oppositions or squares to your client's natal planets. These dates would inform you of any prolonged tertiary or minor progressed stationary aspects. You can then refer back to Chapter Three to see the duration of these progressed aspects.

Endnotes

1. Transit Mars can form three aspects before, during and after retrogradation over a five to six month period. Transit Neptune or Pluto can form five aspects before, during and after two retrograde periods over a 19-20 month period.

Chapter Six
Signs, Degrees, Houses & Angles by Progression

This chapter presents an analysis of progressed planets changing degrees, signs and houses along with the progressed horizon (Ascendant-Descendant axis) and progressed meridian (MC-IC axis) changing degrees and signs. The secondary progressed Moon moving through both the natal and secondary progressed houses concurrently, as well as progressed planets becoming angular will also be discussed. Usage of the astrological decanates, which are 10° subdivisions of each sign, and the dwadashâmshas, which are 2.5° subdivisions of the signs, will be presented as precise interpretive methods of determining your client's current state of awareness of his progressed planets and angles. When preparing for a progressions consultation, I primarily work with aspects, lunations, stations, retrograde planets and house rulerships, but I have gained some valuable insights using the sign, decanate, dwad, degree and house positions of the progressing planets of my clients.

Progressed Sign Ingresses & Degree Analysis

When the secondary, tertiary or minor progressed Sun, Moon or planets change signs, a subtle transition takes place in the personal energy field of the client. In the case of the secondary progressed Sun, for example, which will only change signs two or three times in a normal lifetime, ingress into the following sign represents the beginning of a thirty-year cycle. The astrologer can help the client understand this change by discussing the energetic transitions of fire to earth, earth to air, air to water, or water to fire. The transition of cardinal to fixed, fixed to mutable, or mutable to cardinal can also be highly informative to the client. I have found that sign changes can be more readily understood by the client when I elucidate the mutation taking place as a shift in consciousness based on elemental and modal natural rhythms. I use the phrase "life force sequence" to describe this phenomenon.

When planets in fire signs progress into earth, the three creative impulses are now seeking form, discernment and discipline. Creativity can combust physically (Aries), emotionally (Leo) or intellectually (Sagittarius). The pure creative physical energy of Aries, upon entering the earthy kingdom of Taurus, must now learn to build methodically and pace itself or face exhaustion and risk injury. The pure, creative emotional energy of Leo arriving at the earthy state of Virgo must now discover the technique through which its love can flow. The pure creative mental energy of Sagittarius upon reaching the earthy gates of Capricorn must now perceive how to cultivate abstractions so that they are useful to others.

When planets in earth signs progress into air, the three corporeal states are now seeking social and intellectual connection. Substance can manifest physically (Capricorn), emotionally (Taurus) or intellectually (Virgo). The pure substantive physical energy of Capricorn upon entering the airy realm of Aquarius must now release the pursuit of material status for the knowledge of humane principles. The pure substantive emotional energy of Taurus arriving at the airy dimension of Gemini must now surrender the yoke of self-reliance for an interest in others. The pure substantive mental energy of Virgo reaching the airy province of Libra must now capitulate precise analysis and cerebral categorization for artistic appreciation of beauty and refinement.

When planets in air signs progress into water, the three conceptual spheres are now seeking emotional depth. Ideals can disembark physically (Libra), emotionally (Aquarius) or intellectually (Gemini). The pure idealistic physical energy of Libra entering the watery domain of Scorpio must now yield its poise for the shadowy darkness of irrationality to find purpose. The pure idealistic emotional energy of Aquarius, upon arriving at the watery shores of Pisces, must now abdicate rigid scientific erudition for the great unknown spiritual sea. The pure idealistic mental energy of Gemini reaching the watery placenta of Cancer must now relinquish the naming of environmental factors in lieu of experiencing emotional stratum.

When planets in water signs progress into fire, the three feeling territories are now seeking personal expression. Passion and sympathy can descend physically (Cancer), emotionally (Scorpio) or intellectually (Pisces). The pure sympathetic physical energy of Cancer surfacing at the fiery horizon of Leo must now cede its self-protective armor to the demonstrative flame within. The pure passionate emotional energy of Scorpio transmuting into the fiery plasma of Sagittarius is washed by the blood of the heart through loss in preparation for the rarefied fuel of spiritual perception. The pure sympathetic mental energy of Pisces, upon docking at the fiery wharf of Aries, must now step ashore from a voyage of secretive imagination and courageously lead others through devout personal conviction.

When planets in cardinal signs progress into fixed, a transition occurs from physical reality to the desire plane of consciousness. Needs, feelings and control issues are activated and the personal center of gravity changes. A greater resistance to outside influence is also experienced by the client, as is increased stubbornness, willfulness and inner strength.

When planets in fixed signs progress into mutable, a transition occurs from the desire plane to the mental plane of consciousness. Ideas, conceptual thinking, speculation about possibilities, and detachment from emotional entanglements are activated.

When planets in mutable signs progress into cardinal, a transition occurs from the mental plane to the physical plane of consciousness. Courage, definite courses of action, specific goals and concrete plans are activated. The health may also improve as a result of increased physical activity.

The three current progressed Sun signs and the Sabian symbols for their specific degrees describe an interaction taking place between the three esoteric bodies. The secondary progressed Sun sign and degree is the physical experience, the tertiary progressed Sun sign and degree is the emotional experience, and the minor progressed Sun sign and degree is the mental experience. The relative harmony, or incongruity, of these three signs and their elements, modes, decanates, dwads, degrees and dispositors says a great deal about the level of integration a client may feel at any given point of life.

For example, as I write this chapter (October 1998), I have my secondary progressed Sun at 9° Capricorn (8° 21' rounded up), my tertiary progressed Sun at 17° Cancer, and my minor progressed Sun at 7° Aries. All three Suns are in cardinal signs for me right now, and I am writing a book. I am not just thinking about my book (mutable), nor am I feeling like I want to write my book (fixed), but I am actually doing the work (cardinal). My physical reality, defined by the secondary Sun in 9° Capricorn, is a lot of hard work to succeed at my ambition to share this astrological knowledge about progressions that I have gained through my professional experience.

Interestingly, the Sabian symbol for 9° Capricorn is "An angel carrying a harp." As I am also the owner of a school of astrology, and have a full-time astrology practice, this book is being written between client consultations and teaching classes, workshops and public lectures. In my work with clients recently, I have felt like an angel as I have had the joyful experience of heart-to-heart connection with them. The secondary Sun remains in the same degree for a year, and the Sabian symbol for this degree informs one of the *current physical pattern* being encountered.

My feeling reality, defined by the tertiary Sun in 17° Cancer, is a personal emotional rebirth after an intensely painful relationship and fatherhood loss. I am growing stronger each day as I move forward in my life and recover from the recent past. The Sabian symbol for this degree is "The unfoldment of multilevel potentialities issuing from an original germ," and was described by Rudhyar as "the life urge to actualize one's birth potential." This is precisely what I am feeling these days, as I struggle to climb out of the emotional immaturity of my Cancer South Node, and into the responsibilities of personal accomplishment I am capable of through my Capricorn North Node. The tertiary Sun, which progresses about

13 1/3 degrees per year, will thus remain in the same degree for about 27- 28 days, and the Sabian symbol for this degree specifically informs one of the *current emotional pattern* being encountered.

My thinking reality, defined by the minor Sun in 7° Aries, is an awareness that I can make a creative contribution to the astrological community through my writing, even as I struggle to grow stronger again in my personal life through the courage to be alone. The Sabian symbol for this degree is "A man succeeds in expressing himself simultaneously in two realms." This symbol speaks to my present realization that I can travel, like an angel, between the two worlds that I live in. When there is time to write, I am happy to again travel from the realm of client work and the usage of these progression techniques into the metaphysical realm that allows me to perceive and explain to you how and why progressions work. The minor Sun, which progresses about 27 1/3 degrees per year, will remain in the same degree for about a fortnight; the Sabian symbol for this degree speaks to the *current mental pattern* being encountered.

The astrologer, when working with the current progressed signs and degrees of the three different sets of Sun, Moon and planets, needs to remember the relative importance, based on duration, of the secondaries, tertiaries and minors. These degree analysis techniques can be likened to a sort of "metaphysical horary" astrology where the astrologer is trying to respond to the immediate needs of a client who has an upset and requires a daily, weekly or monthly spiritual perspective to help cope with what he is going through. The minor progressed Moon, for example, travels about a degree per day, and thus, has a Sabian symbol that explains the memories (Moon) that are surfacing mentally (minor progression). By tomorrow, the client will be in the next degree of the minor Moon, and, therefore, the depth of identification with the degree symbol is obviously transitory. If a client is distraught, depressed or suicidal, an explanation of this passing spiritual reality can offer comfort in a dark hour.

The most important progressed planet sign changes occur in the secondaries since a lengthy chapter of life is concluding and a new one beginning. The astrologer needs to be careful when "eyeballing" the length of secondary progressed Mercury, Venus or Mars in a sign since full orbital motion, mean orbital motion, or stationary orbital motion will affect the length of progressed sign duration.

The secondary progressed Sun remains in a sign for about 30 years, the secondary Moon for about two to two and-one-half years. Secondary Mercury *averages* 21 years in a sign (unless stationing), secondary Venus remains in a sign for about 25 years (unless stationing), and secondary Mars for about 40 years (unless stationing). After calculating the derived date for the client's secondary progressions, a glance at the ephemeris will locate any sign ingresses about to occur. This is preferable to sole reliance on a computer-calculated bi-wheel or tri-wheel chart, as a planet may be in a late degree and *look like it is about to change signs* when, in fact, it is approaching a station and will still remain in that sign for years to come in retrograde motion.

I have recently experienced my Venus secondary progress from Sagittarius into Capricorn, ending a 24-year chapter in my life. With a natal Venus-Saturn conjunction in the second house, I feel like I am back in familiar territory again. I would say that the progressing Venus in Sagittarius correlated with several risk-taking plunges into personal relationships that proved disastrous for me, but, nonetheless, have been my advanced education (Sagittarius) in the school of love (Venus). I also had as a common denominator with the women I was closest to a shared spiritual path or religious conviction. Now, for example, with Venus having progressed into Capricorn, I find myself thoroughly enjoying the social sweetness of the elderly couples I encounter at the local Theosophical Society lodge, where I give lectures on esoteric astrology. To listen to an 80-year old dear spiritual sister play Mozart on the piano with nimble fingers and a heart of gold must qualify for Venus in Capricorn heaven.

I have noted my client's secondary progressed planets having had recent sign changes and during consultation, have inquired about the realm of life associated with that particular planet. One client recently had her secondary Venus progress from Aquarius into Pisces. Within the first year of this occurrence, her entire social circle completely changed from political and environmental activists to artists, poets, musicians and dancers. She owns a clothing boutique here in my town, and a Middle East belly dance studio opened up next door. But wait, there's more. She's hosting poetry readings at her store.

Another client who recently came in for a progressions consultation just had her secondary progressed Sun leave Gemini and enter Cancer, ending a 30-year cycle. She has a natal Taurus Sun, a Leo Moon. The only significant water in her birthchart by sign is Saturn in Scorpio. She left to travel a few days before the progressed sign change was going to be exact, knowing that, while she was gone, a brother who was being released from prison after eight years would be coming to her house and taking the furniture she had been using all those years. Her husband, meanwhile, ordered new furniture, to be delivered while she was gone. Her secondary Sun had left Gemini and entered Cancer while she was away, and when she arrived home, she had a complete emotional reaction (Cancer) to the new furnishings. It was a personal response she had never experienced before, crying almost inconsolably. In her own words, she said that she thought furniture was furniture, and mostly utilitarian and functional, and she never could have imagined reacting like that. Welcome to the water element, my friend.

Clients educate me daily with their real-life experiences of progressing planets changing signs. I could not make up these stories if I tried.

To summarize, the astrologer should pay the most attention to any secondary progressed sign changes of the Sun, Moon, Mercury, Venus or Mars. The three current progressed Sun signs should be analyzed, along with a reading of the Sabian symbols for each of the current progressed Sun degrees. Tertiary planets changing signs will affect the feelings, and minor progressed planets changing signs will primarily alter the thoughts.

If you have daily contact with a client who is working through pain, depression or confusion, I recommend calculating the minor progressed Moon. This changes a degree per day and the Sabian symbol for each degree change can offer comfort and guidance.

If you are doing more extensive work with a client, such as a series of weekly appointments where you are presenting a retrospective account of his life (water signs love this), as seen through the history of their progressions, then in addition to researching the lunation cycles, stations, retrogrades and aspects, be sure to calculate all the dates of the secondary, tertiary and minor progressed Sun, Moon (exclude tertiary/minor), Mercury, Venus and Mars sign changes. Arrange these in chronological order and explain them as the personal energy field transitions the client has experienced which are dated in time. These sign changes will be the turning of the pages of the story of the client's life.

Progressed Angularity & House Ingresses

As in all other astrological calculations, progressed angular planets are given supreme importance. This is so because when a planet transits or progresses from a cadent house into an angular house, what had existed only in thought form (cadent), now comes into physical manifestation (angular), and "stuff happens." The only exceptions that I have observed to this astrological rule are the transit lunar nodes, which, as you know, move retrograde through the Zodiac in an 18 and one-half year cycle. Therefore, the transit lunar nodes move from angular houses into cadent houses, and often, I have noticed, represent lost opportunities. If the client did not act on the spiritual urge to grow and make changes while the transit nodes were in angular houses, I have watched the impulse recede through the cadent and succedent houses, only to reappear when the transit nodes again become angular.

Secondary progressed planets becoming angular will coincide with life's most obvious structural changes. The secondary Moon, in particular, just about always correlates, within a month or two, with major life change when angular. The tertiary progressed Moon, which has a 24 and one-half month cycle through the horoscope houses, is also important to watch when angular. What is also very much worth researching is when progressed planets are angular using the *secondary progressed angles*. I used to think that only the natal houses were important in progressions, but I am thoroughly convinced now that clients experience life on two levels of house reality—the natal and the progressed houses each representing a different sphere.

A basic metaphysical rule in understanding this phenomenon is that when working with progressions, the natal houses define the external, concrete areas of life while the secondary progressed houses define the inner, spiritual progress taking place. In *The Progressed Horoscope*, Alan Leo made the same observation, stating:

> "The native may be regarded as having, in effect, two personalities—the hereditary or root temperament and disposition he was born with, and the modification or outgrowth thereof that he has evolved for himself from the former by the play of his thought and will upon the physical environment he found himself placed in. The former will remain unaffected except by such influences as disturb the radix or nativity, the latter will be amenable (more or less, according to the progressive character of the soul) to every modification of the progressed horoscope."

In my opinion, what Alan Leo was saying is that the progressed houses represent the current state of spiritual evolution for the client as a result of experiences thus far in life, while the natal houses define the more routine environmental influences in life.

For example, currently my secondary progressed Moon is in my natal second house, and simultaneously in my progressed twelfth house. I am experiencing my life on these two levels as such: my *natal* second house progressed Moon is requiring me to rebuild the income in my astrological business (school and practice), after having been away from the area for two and a half years. My progressed Moon has been in the *progressed* twelfth house for the last two and a half years, and has resulted in a thorough emotional and spiritual cleansing for me, with the deepest loss and pain I have ever experienced in my life, yet, at the same time, awakening my deepest sympathetic emotions, universal love for others, and, most importantly, taking me through a heart journey into a spiritual rebirth that I could have never imagined.

Planets progressing out of the natal or progressed 12th house and crossing the ascendant into the natal or progressed 1st house are experienced as having successfully passed through a long, dark night of the soul, making it to the light of dawn. Minor or tertiary progressed planets leaving the 12th house and becoming angular on the ascendant usually correlate with a mental or emotional dilemma having been overcome, such as depression, despair, or paralyzing fear, anxiety and worry. These angular progressions represent the journey from the water element into the fire element, and thus, normally produce two spiritual baptisms: one of water, where one is purified through sorrow and atonement, and one of fire, where one can receive the descent of the Holy Spirit into the flame of the personal heart, giving the courage to now be strong for others.

The minor progressed Sun, which travels about 27-28 degrees per year, will usually spend over a year in the 12th house, while the tertiary progressed Sun, which moves about 13 degrees per year, will normally spend over two years in the 12th house. These will test one's faith at the deepest levels. After crossing the ascendant, ideally, renewed confidence results from greater spiritual integration since one has experienced the entire range of mental and emotional doubts and come through.

Other than the Moon, secondary progressed planets leaving the 12th house and becoming angular on the ascendant do not always necessarily coincide with an *immediate* change in the quality of life. There may have to be several trials and errors before the client leaves behind the residue of isolation, reclusivity and loneliness and *fully* shows up for life in the "real" world. The astrologer can view this as if observing an alcoholic in recovery, one day feeling strong, the next day feeling on the brink of relapse. Clients need encouragement in approaching the 12th house-1st house transition *gradually*, while honoring where their spiritual journey has taken them.

Progressing planets crossing the natal or progressed IC from the 3rd house into the 4th house, will often coincide with some of the more karmic family events such as finding a lost parent after having been adopted out, the birth of children, death of a parent, or recollection of childhood trauma previously unconscious. These angular progressions represent the journey from the air element into the water element, and thus, normally produce an initiation into the emotional self. As the ancestral genetic DNA code is symbolically transferred into the soul through the IC, these angular progressions sometimes also coincide with the discovery of hereditary illnesses, be they mental or physiological.

Progressing planets crossing the natal or progressed descendant from the 6th house into the 7th house quite often coincide with relationship beginnings or endings. As the progressing planet climbs above the horizon, the client may feel as if he is coming out of a phase of inner development into a more visible worldly role. These angular progressions represent the journey from the earth element into the air element, and thus, generally produce an increased objective awareness of oneself, usually through the feedback from others, or the fully illumined grasp of the larger purpose of one's life.

Progressing planets crossing the natal or progressed MC from the 9th house into the 10th house will often coincide with some professional achievement or recognition, the start of a business or professional practice, a significant promotion, or a career change. As the progressing planet culminates, the client may experience the feeling of having reached the top of the mountain after a long and tedious climb. I have also seen the secondary progressed Moon, when angular at the MC, coincide with the completion of graduate school and the start of a new career for the client. These angular progressions represent the journey from the fire element into the earth element, and, therefore, the building of form around the vision.

While planets progressing from natal or progressed angular houses into succedent houses, or from natal or progressed succedent houses into cadent houses, are not as significant as progressed planets becoming angular, in the case of the secondaries, they do represent a lengthy chapter of life coming to completion, and a new one beginning. When this occurs, the astrologer should make note of this and explain it to the client.

Metaphysically speaking, from angular to succedent is quite similar to the passage from cardinal to fixed, where there is a transition from physical reality into the desire plane of consciousness. The astrologer can better understand this esoteric phenomenon by investigating the four gates in their own birthchart which lead into this desire plane, and these are the specific degrees of the succedent 2nd, 5th, 8th and 11th house cusps. By studying the Sabian symbols of these degrees for one's own birthchart, the astrologer is in a better position to articulate this passage to the client. This technique will also apply to the cusp degrees of the cadent 3rd, 6th, 9th and 12th houses, as these are the gates between the desire plane of consciousness and the mental plane.

The Progressed Horizon & Meridian

When working with the progressed angles in astrology, the time of birth is obviously essential for accuracy. Progressing the ascendant and midheaven can actually be used to rectify a birthchart where the time is either unknown or suspect. As you know, the angles move about a degree every four minutes of clock time, and even in the case of a horoscope only ten minutes off, this can result in a progressed MC that is two and one-half degrees, or two and a half years from accuracy. If the astrologer does not have the skills to rectify a suspect birth time, he should limit his work with progressions to the planets only, and leave the angles alone.

Personally, I only have experience working with the secondary progressed angles in my practice. I have not extensively investigated the Quotidian, or daily, angles normally used with tertiary and minor progression calculations as these only reflect the angularity of the derived progressed date and time, and to me, do not appear to be directly linked to the spiritual evolution of the client's natal ascendant and midheaven. I have seen such exact life experience coincidence with the secondary progressed angles in close aspect to natal planets, that I have never found it necessary to look beyond the secondary progressed ascendant or MC.

I have researched the solar arc, Naibod arc, Ptolemaic arc, and Massey arc methods for progressing the MC in my work with my clients. The Solar Arc method advances the natal MC the same number of longitudinal degrees and minutes as the secondary progressed Sun. There is a variation on this method which is to advance the MC by solar arc in right ascension, rather than by longitude. Right ascension is the measurement eastwards around the equator from 0° Aries. The difference between the two is often fractional (a few minutes of arc).

The Naibod arc method advances the natal MC 0° 59' 08" in longitude per year, which is the mean daily motion of the Sun. There is also the optional calculation of Naibod arc in right ascension. Between the Naibod and Solar Arc (in longitude) progression of the MC, there can be a several degree (± 5°) difference by the age of 60 for a client born around the winter solstice when the Sun moves at its greatest daily orbital motion. This degree difference is critical, as the *progressed ascendant is derived from the progressed MC.*

The Ptolemaic arc method advances the natal MC 1° of right ascension per year, and does not correspond with either the actual or mean daily motion of the Sun. The Massey method of MC progression is a variation on this, where the MC is advanced 1° of longitude per year.

Earlier in my practice, when I was confronted with not only which MC progression calculation to use but also with the choice between natal or relocated latitude and longitude, I asked how I was going to prove to myself which is accurate? I began to notice that the dates of commencement of the most important personal relationships for my clients nearly always coincided with something going on with the progressed ascendant (aspect or sign change).

Since there are mind-rattling numbers of ways to calculate the secondary progressed ascendant, I decided once and for all to test these calculations. I progressed the MC six different ways (two solar arcs, two Naibods, one Ptolemaic, one Massey), using either natal or relocated latitudes, giving twelve different progressed ascendants. I found exact correlations between the dates of new relationships (the day of the first meeting of a husband or wife or true love) entering the client's life, and the progressed ascendant changing signs, or being in nearly partile aspect to a natal planet, using the *solar arc in longitude method to progress the MC, and natal latitude to determine the progressed ascendant.* I found in some cases that this coincided to the day.

The significance of the progressed ascendant cannot be overestimated in astrology. Metaphysically, it represents the changing personal horizon as the client goes through life, separating the inner self from the outer self, the lower world of darkness from the upper world of light. In my opinion, the ascendant is the single most spiritual point in the horoscope, simply because it is so time-sensitive (moving a degree, on average, every four minutes).

The Sabian symbol for the natal ascendant, I have found, is the one that clients most identify with. The degree of the progressing ascendant, and its Sabian symbol, illustrate the *current* spiritual integration taking place for the client. This integration can be symbolically viewed as the marriage of the shadow self (below the horizon) with the conscious self (above the horizon). This reason alone is why I have exclusively worked with the secondary progressed ascendant, and not the Quotidian angles.

The astrologer has to be extra careful when attempting to "eyeball" the progressed ascendant. You can get away with adding the client's age to the degree of the natal MC, and be pretty close to the progressed MC, but you will make a fool out of yourself if you attempt to do this with the progressed ascendant. The reason for this is, because of the 23 1/2° tilt of the earth's polar axis, there are signs of short ascension and signs of long ascension. The natal midheaven and ascendant are rarely at a right angle to each other, and rarely does the progressed ascendant advance at the same rate of speed as the progressed MC. The net result of all this is that sometimes the progressed ascendant will have moved a greater number of degrees than the progressed MC, and sometimes fewer.

For example, my natal MC is 20° 45' Gemini, and my natal ascendant is 21° 30' Virgo. As I write, my progressed MC is at 6° 23' Leo, and my progressed ascendant is at 2° 28' Scorpio. As you can see, at my age (45 in 1998), my MC has progressed almost 46°, and my ascendant has progressed almost 41°. This is only a differential of 5° but I have calculated progressed charts of clients who had a differential of over 25-35° between the MC and ascendant at my age.

Recently, I had a client whose natal ascendant was 16° Pisces, and natal MC was 22° Sagittarius. At the age of 46, the ascendant had progressed to 28° Taurus, some 72°, while the midheaven had progressed to 7° Aquarius, only 45°, thus giving a difference of 27°. Another client had a natal ascendant of 5° Aquarius, and a natal MC of 28° Scorpio. The ascendant had progressed to 25° Aries at the age of 45, some 80°, while the progressed MC was 13° Capricorn, only 45°, thus, giving a difference of 35°. The point is, don't try to "guesstimate" the progressed ascendant by adding the age of the client to the natal ascendant, or, in the case of rising signs of short ascension (Aquarius, Pisces and Aries in the northern hemisphere), you could be off by over 30° by mid-life, and make a remark about some presumed progressed ascendant conjunction to a natal planet (which I have seen several astrologers do), and not even be on the map.

The progressed midheaven is extraordinarily important in astrology, as it also reflects the evolving spiritual integration of the client, as does the progressed ascendant, but more socially and professionally. Metaphysically, it is the changing personal meridian (north-south axis) as one goes through life, separating the self-aware "I" from the projection of the "not I" or "you" onto others. Each year, the client gets a new pair of degrees for both the secondary progressed MC and IC. The Sabian symbols for these degrees represent the spiritual polarity taking place between the evolving personal unconscious (progressed IC) and the evolution of one's place in the world (progressed MC). The current degree of the progressed MC can be described as a projection onto the screen of one's social reputation, of the breeding, training and genetic inheritances from the family that are bearing fruit, and also of any strength of character gained through personal emotional chaos, loss and recovery.

The astrologer should also note if a client's secondary progressed ascendant or midheaven is changing signs. This will occur at least three times for either angle during a normal lifetime (four or five times with rising signs of short ascension), and thus, is as important as the secondary Sun changing signs. What is critical to remember is that, as the progressing angles change signs, one gets *new planetary rulers*, and the *natal condition* (sign strength, retrogradation, house position or aspect) of these planetary rulers is essential for correct analysis of the progressed angles. I have repeatedly seen the date of the progressed ascendant changing signs, or forming a conjunction or opposition with a natal planet coinciding with an important personal relationship entering the life. As I mentioned earlier, this was the technique I used to test all the different methods of progressing the MC, for the progressed ascendant is derived from the progressed midheaven, using either the natal or relocated latitude.

When the progressed MC changes signs—about every 30 years—the clients will "change costumes" out in the world, while still remaining themselves personally. The astrologer can look at the progressed MC as the *intended* destiny of the client at any given point in life, and from the response the client has to the meaning inherent within the Sabian symbol for the current degree of the progressed MC, the astrologer can tell how spiritually aligned the client is with his higher self.

As I send this little book out into the world to you, my progressed MC is in the 7th degree of Leo, for which the Sabian symbol is "The constellations of stars shine brilliantly in the night sky." As a career astrologer, and one who has been trying to write his first book for many years, I see how things hinge on timing. Deep in my heart, I am happy that now is the time for me to make my creative contribution to the astrological community.

Using Decanates & Dwadashâmshas in Progressions

A valuable technique to aid understanding of the meaning of the current progressed planets or angles is the subdivision of the signs into 10° decanates, or 2.5° dwadashâmshas, commonly known as "dwads." The dwads are a Hindu technique of sign subdivision imported to the west from India. By no means are they limited to the sidereal Zodiac. Tropical astrologers can certainly employ the dwad system of sign subdivision as effectively as any Vedic astrologer.

The esoteric concept behind the systems of sign division is that each sign contains the entire Zodiac within it. This is akin to the theory of fractals wherein the whole pattern is contained within any of its parts. In Chapter Four, I wrote about the "holographic time links" that explain how the secondary progressed lunations are directly connected to the earlier-in-life tertiary or minor progressed lunations. These links illustrate how specific chapters of childhood correlate with specific chapters of adult life. In the twelve days between Christmas and Epiphany, for example, the followers of the Anthroposophical teachings of Rudolph Steiner believe that each month of the new year is contained in miniature in each of these twelve days. According to this theory, these sacred days from December 25th until January 6th are the days one should sincerely make spiritual resolutions for improvement for the year.

What is spiritually revealed to the esoteric astrologer through the decanates and dwads is the mystery of hidden planetary rulerships. As planets move through the degrees of the signs, there is a continual change of concealed rulership that takes place. The decanates, breaking the 30° signs into three 10° subdivisions, assign a sub-influence of the two other signs of the same element, along with a planetary rulership sub-influence.

The dwads take this one step further by breaking each 10° decanate into four 2.5° sign subdivisions. For example, 00° 01' to 10° 00' of Aries is the Aries decanate, and has pure Mars rulership. 10° 01' to 20° 00' Aries is the Leo (succeeding fire sign) decanate, and has a Mars-Sun rulership. 20° 01' to 30° 00' Aries is the Sagittarius decanate, with a Mars-Jupiter rulership. The Aries decanate of Aries contains the Aries, Taurus, Gemini and Cancer dwads. The Leo decanate of Aries contains the Leo, Virgo, Libra and Scorpio dwads. The Sagittarius decanate of Aries contains the Sagittarius, Capricorn, Aquarius and Pisces dwads.

The astrologer, when attempting to interpret the progressed ascendant and midheaven of his client, can always refer to the Sabian symbol for the current degree of the two progressed angles. But, there is additional insight that can be gained from an investigation into the decanate, dwad and planetary rulerships.

For example, my progressed MC is currently at 6° 23' Leo. This degree places my progressed midheaven into the Leo decanate, Libra (5° 01' to 7° 30') dwad, and gives it a Sun-Venus subrulership. I have been trying for the last 10 and one-half months to put all the love (Venus) I have in my heart (Sun) into writing this book, and the creative spark for its inception was the birth of a daughter (Venus) who, as an infant, I watched as her mother taught ballet (Venus) classes to children (Sun), while my daughter slept in a pink (Venus) pajama jumpsuit in a battery operated swing in a shed I used as an office on the Oregon coast as I began to write.

At this point, I could do no better than refer the reader to Alan Leo's *The Progressed Horoscope*, where in Chapter XII he writes extensively on the progressed ascendant, employing these techniques to delineate the three subdivisions of each progressed rising sign, broken down by decanate. You will find that he used the traditional rulerships of Mars for Scorpio, Jupiter for Pisces, and Saturn for Aquarius to arrive at his interpretations of the Scorpio, Pisces or Aquarius decanates of any the rising signs in these same elements. I would be hard pressed to reach anything near the level of insight he had while defining the subtleties of each of the progressing ascendants.

I would encourage all my readers to employ these techniques of sign subdivision while working with the progressed angles for your clients. To activate your perceptions, I recommend the following experiential exercise for you: Take three of your clients who have the same rising sign, but in different decanates. For example, one has a 6° Virgo ascendant, another a 16° Virgo ascendant, and a third, a 26° Virgo ascendant. Then, determine the decanate, dwad and planetary rulers of these natal ascendants; i.e. 6° Virgo = Mercury-Mars (Virgo decanate, Scorpio dwad), 16° Virgo = Mercury-Saturn-Jupiter (Capricorn decanate, Pisces dwad), and 26° Virgo = Mercury-Venus-Moon (Taurus decanate, Cancer dwad).

Next, recollect their energy mentally, or call them on the phone, say you are doing research, and talk to them for a little while. Or better yet, invite them to lunch, where you can observe them directly. Paying attention to their personal energy field, see if you can perceive the different planetary subrulers interacting. I assure you that, with trained perception, you can distinctly see these influences at work. Of course, the chart ruler by sign, house and aspect is also seen clearly through the ascendant, but, so too are the decanates, dwads and planetary subrulers if you look for them.

The following table shows each of the twelve signs, along with their decanates and dwads.

Table 13 - Decanates and Dwadashâmshas

Sign	♈	♉	♊	♋	♌	♍	♎	♏	♐	♑	♒	♓
0° to 10°	♈	♉	♊	♋	♌	♍	♎	♏	♐	♑	♒	♓
0° to 2.5°	♈	♉	♊	♋	♌	♍	♎	♏	♐	♑	♒	♓
2.5° to 5°	♉	♊	♋	♌	♍	♎	♏	♐	♑	♒	♓	♈
5° to 7.5°	♊	♋	♌	♍	♎	♏	♐	♑	♒	♓	♈	♉
7.5° to 10°	♋	♌	♍	♎	♏	♐	♑	♒	♓	♈	♉	♊
10° to 20°	♌	♍	♎	♏	♐	♑	♒	♓	♈	♉	♊	♋
10° to 12.5°	♌	♍	♎	♏	♐	♑	♒	♓	♈	♉	♊	♋
12.5° to 15°	♍	♎	♏	♐	♑	♒	♓	♈	♉	♊	♋	♌
15° to 17.5°	♎	♏	♐	♑	♒	♓	♈	♉	♊	♋	♌	♍
17.5° to 20°	♏	♐	♑	♒	♓	♈	♉	♊	♋	♌	♍	♎
20° to 30°	♐	♑	♒	♓	♈	♉	♊	♋	♌	♍	♎	♏
20° to 22.5°	♐	♑	♒	♓	♈	♉	♊	♋	♌	♍	♎	♏
22.5° to 25°	♑	♒	♓	♈	♉	♊	♋	♌	♍	♎	♏	♐
25° to 27.5°	♒	♓	♈	♉	♊	♋	♌	♍	♎	♏	♐	♑
27.5° to 30°	♓	♈	♉	♊	♋	♌	♍	♎	♏	♐	♑	♒

Endnotes

1. I recommend using geocentric, in lieu of geographic, latitudes for natal and progressed calculations. You will find this option in your astrology software atlas preferences.

Chapter Seven
Discerning Significant Progressed Aspects
Preparing for the Client Consultation

As I mentioned in Chapter One, preparing for a progressions consultation confronts the astrologer with a myriad of various progressed-to-natal, progressed-to-progressed, transit-to-natal, and transit-to-progressed aspects. In addition, house position, house ruler activation, lunations, eclipses, stations, retrogrades, angles, decanates, dwads and degrees expands this list even further. Out of this vast maze of planetary activity, the experienced astrologer knows exactly what to look for, and thus, how to discern which of the progressed or transiting aspects are more important, and which are of lesser importance. In this chapter are techniques that I use to extract the most significant planetary activity taking place for the client.

In all cases of progressed or transit activity, I recommend using *very tight orbs*. This means 1° applying, and 1/2° to 1° separating. You will be much more successful in your work with progressions if you discipline yourself to only consider aspect activity within this limited orb allowance. For the sake of brevity, references to progressed houses in this chapter are to the secondary progressed houses, calculated with a progressed MC using solar arc in longitude, and the natal latitude to produce the progressed ascendant. I recommend the Porphyry house division system for work with progressions. In this system the quadrants are trisected, producing equally sized houses within each quadrant. Before a consultation, I calculate the following charts and reports:

1. A natal-secondary progressed-transit tri-wheel chart
2. Secondary progressed chart with progressed houses
3. A natal-tertiary progressed bi-wheel chart
4. A natal-minor progressed bi-wheel chart
5. Secondary progressed to natal aspect report
6. Transit to secondary progressed aspect report
7. Transit to natal aspect report

Orienting Yourself to the Client's Longer Cycles

Starting with the tri-wheel chart, I note the various progressed and transit activity I see. To orient myself to the client's long-term cycles, I make a note of the current secondary progressed Sun-Moon phase (29.5 year cycle), the current phase of the Saturn transit cycle (29.5 years) to its natal position, and the current phase of the Jupiter transit cycle (12 years) to its natal position. Next, I make a note of transit Jupiter and Saturn by house, hemisphere and quadrant. Then, I note both the natal and progressed house positions of the secondary Moon.

Next I research the phase entry degree of the current secondary progressed Sun-Moon phase. For example, if the client is in the secondary lunation gibbous phase, I find the precise degree of the secondary Moon as it formed a waxing sesquiquadrate to the secondary Sun. Then I research the specific degree of the previous progressed New Moon, and if the lunation cycle is waning, the degree of the previous progressed Full Moon. I also note the degree of the previous Quarter Moon. I then make notes about the Sabian symbols for these lunation degrees. If either the New Moon or Full Moon was also an eclipse, this gets underlined.

Progressed Moon Aspects

Following up with my investigation into the secondary Moon, I look for any progressed to natal aspects forming within six months of the consultation date along with any sign or house changes. If the natal Moon also aspects any of the same planets that the secondary Moon will be aspecting, I underline these. For example, if the client has a natal Moon-Saturn trine and the secondary Moon is moving into a conjunction with natal Saturn, this is specifically noted. If the secondary Moon will be crossing over, or opposing, the degree of a forming progressed to natal aspect, a transit to natal aspect, or a transit to progressed aspect, I double-underline this. I also note if the secondary Moon is approaching angularity.

Next, I make notes about the current phases of both the tertiary and minor progressed Moons. The tertiary lunation cycle lasts for 24 and one-half months, and the minor lunation cycle lasts for one year. I research the specific degree and Sabian symbol of the previous tertiary and minor New Moons, and if either is waning, I also note the degree of the previous Full Moon. Again, as with the secondary Moon, I note if any New or Full Moons were also eclipses. I also look to see if the degree of any current tertiary or minor New, Quarter or Full Moons matches a degree of any of the lifetime secondary lunation degrees.

Progressed Sun Aspects

Then I jump into an analysis of the three progressed Suns. I make a note of the secondary, tertiary and minor progressed Sun signs, decanates, dwads and individual degrees, making a special note if a sign or house change is occurring. If there are aspects between the progressed Suns and the natal Sun, I note this. For example, the natal Sun is at 22° Scorpio, and the tertiary Sun is at 21° Cancer and moving into a waning trine with the natal Sun, the date of this occurrence is added to the list. I also research where the tertiary and minor Suns are in respect to phase with the natal Sun. The tertiary Sun has a 27 1/3 year cycle through the natal houses before returning to a conjunction with the natal Sun. I make a note of what phase it currently is in, and when the next eighth harmonic (phase change) aspect will occur. The minor Sun has a 13 1/3 year cycle through the natal houses, and I also make notes about its current phase, and when its next eighth harmonic aspect to the natal Sun will occur.

Next, I look to see if the secondary Sun is forming any aspect with a natal planet or angle. And I mean *any aspect*. In my opinion, these secondary progressed Sun aspects are the most important of any aspect activity occurring at any given time. Obviously, any "A" team aspects (conjunction, opposition, trine or square) are most important. "B" team aspects (semisextile, semisquare, sextile, sesquiquadrate or quincunx) are next in importance. Any "C" team aspects (undecile, decile, novile, septile, quintile or their derived multiples of biquintile, triseptile, etc.) would be of lesser importance, but since they involve the secondary Sun, they certainly would inform the astrologer of any subtle spiritual evolution taking place.

Continuing, I scrutinize the tertiary and minor progressed Suns, making a note of their current natal and progressed house positions. I list any conjunctions or oppositions from the tertiary or minor Sun to any natal planet, and if either Sun is approaching angularity.

Progressed Ascendant & Midheaven Aspects

From here, I turn my attention to the progressed ascendant and MC. I note the current pair of degrees for the progressed horizon (ASC-DSC) and for the progressed meridian (MC-IC), along with their respective Sabian symbols. I make a note of the current decanate and dwad of both the progressed rising sign and the progressed MC sign, along with their planetary subrulerships. I recommend using the traditional rulerships of Mars for Scorpio, Jupiter for Pisces, and Saturn for Aquarius when working with decanate and dwad planetary subrulers.

Following this, I look for any aspects that will form from the progressed angles to natal planets. I consider conjunctions and oppositions together, as a conjunction forming from the progressed ascendant to natal Saturn will also simultaneously create an opposition from the progressed descendant to natal Saturn. I have observed the progressed angles forming squares to natal planets to be significant, but not so much the trines and sextiles. However, I have found the quincunx from the progressed ascendant or MC to a natal planet to be of high impact, usually with some stress-related health problems resulting from relational tension (progressed ASC-DSC) or family/career dilemmas (progressed MC-IC).

I also make a note of any parans where there is simultaneous progressed angularity occurring with two planets. For example, the progressed MC is forming a conjunction with natal Uranus while the progressed ascendant is forming a conjunction with natal Neptune. If the astrologer finds a paran by progression, it is almost certain that the entire structure of the client's life will be transformed in a fashion relevant to the two planets involved.

Progressed Mercury, Venus & Mars Aspects & Retrogradation

Next, I look for any aspects between secondary progressed personal planets and natal planets or angles. I put conjunctions, oppositions and squares at the top of this part of the list, with trines and quincunxes next in relative importance. After these aspects are listed, I place any other aspects, such as sextiles, semisquares, etc. into a separate category.

From here, I examine secondary, tertiary and minor progressed Mercury, Venus, or Mars for retrogradation. If so, I research the retrograde stationary date and degree, when the progressed direct station will occur and in what degree. Inspecting the retrograde degree span, I look for any aspect between a natal planet or angle while retrograde. If so, it will be a "triple aspect" and I research the dates of the first and third aspects of the set. Most importantly, I look for any progressed planetary station that has or will occur while within a one degree orb of aspecting a natal planet or angle. This phenomenon produces the prolonged stationary aspects mentioned in Chapters Three and Five.

Next, are secondary, tertiary or minor progressed Mercury, Venus or Mars experiencing a sign ingress shortly, becoming angular, or crossing intermediate house cusps? If so, research the dates and make note of them.

Investigating the tertiary and minor progressed Mercury cycles, I note the phase relationship between progressed Mercury and natal Mercury. Tertiary Mercury has 26 3/4 year cycle through the natal houses, while minor Mercury has a 13 1/8 year cycle. I also make a note of the date of the next eighth harmonic aspect occurring between progressed and natal Mercury. Then, I repeat these steps for Venus and Mars. Tertiary Venus has either a 22 and one-half year or 30 year cycle through the natal houses, depending on whether or not retrogradation occurs during a cycle. Minor Venus has either a 10 3/4 year or 14 3/4 year cycle through the natal houses, again depending on whether retrogradation occurred. Tertiary Mars has a 53 year cycle, and minor Mars has a 26 year cycle through the natal houses. As with Mercury, I note the four current phase relationships between the progressed Venus and Mars to their natal positions.

Progressed Jupiter & Saturn Aspects & Retrogradation

While the client won't live long enough to experience complete progressed cycles of Jupiter or Saturn through the natal houses, in a normal life span he will undergo several tertiary or minor progressed stations and retrograde periods of these planets. If these retrograde degree spans form aspects to natal planets or angles, then the triple aspect phenomenon will occur. If the stationary degrees of progressed Jupiter or Saturn form an aspect to a natal planet or angle, then the prolonged stationary aspect phenomenon will occur.

After looking at secondary progressed Jupiter and Saturn and determining if any aspects or stations are occurring, I also pay attention to whether or not natal Jupiter or Saturn reversed direction by progression earlier in life. If so, I research to see at what age this occurred and when the progressed planet would have formed the conjunction to the natal position. For example, I recently had a client whose natal Jupiter was retrograde at 11° Taurus. At the age of 19, secondary progressed Jupiter went stationary direct and his family moved from the U.S. to Australia. At the age of 38, progressed Jupiter finally reached the direct motion conjunction with natal Jupiter. I explained this latter occurrence to the client as a turning point in his life giving him the freedom to define success for himself on his own terms (he was separating himself from involvement in a family business at the time.) Likewise, if the natal Jupiter or Saturn was direct, then progressed into retrograde motion, the date of the retrograde conjunction to the natal position would also be significant as a major turning point in life.

I also make notes of whether tertiary or minor progressed Jupiter and Saturn are currently direct or retrograde, when the last station was, in what degree, and what the Sabian symbol was. As mentioned earlier, tertiary Jupiter remains retrograde for about 9 years, with about 20-21 years between retrogradation. Minor Jupiter remains retrograde for about 4 and one-half years, with about 10 years between retrogradation. Tertiary Saturn retrogrades for about 10 and one-half years, with about 18 years between retrograde periods, and minor Saturn remains retrograde for about 5 years, with about 8 and one-half years between retrogradation.

These direct and retrograde periods of tertiary and minor progressed Jupiter or Saturn can be seen as the metaphysical equivalents to the blood and backbone of life. The astrologer can view the direct and retrograde stations as the bookends of the different chapters in life. Personal growth, risk-taking, pursuit of aspirations, self-improvement, spiritual seeking and travel are continually held in balance by failure, loss, rejection, pain, experience, limitations and atonement. The self-referencing of retrogradation is successively tested by the societal approval or disapproval of direct motion. This inward and outward dance of Jupiter and Saturn by tertiary and minor progression can be viewed by the astrologer as the spiritual ebb and flow of the entire life. It is my opinion that these progressed cycles are distinctly more informative than the outer planet transits, but a certain subtlety of perception is required to appreciate their relevance.

Transits to Progressed Planets

After making notes of all the progressed activity, I investigate the transit aspects, house positions and house activation taking place. In my experience, transits to progressed planets operate in one sphere of reality, while transits to natal planets operate in another. I have found that the transit conjunctions, oppositions or squares to the natal planets often function as house activators, where the natal planet being transited, through its rulership of the sign on the cusp of a house(s), creates disruption or change in that area of life. The transit-to-natal experience of the client is one of *reaction to what is occurring.* Of greater value in my opinion, are transits to progressed planets which tend to help in spiritually integrating what has already happened externally.

In most cases, I find that a natal pair of planets which aspect one another and have then moved into a subsequent progressed aspect, while simultaneously undergoing a transit-to-natal or transit-to-progressed trigger by one of the same two planets, coincide with the most lasting changes and transformations in life.

For example, I recently had a client, a 66 year-old physician, who had natal Mercury at 22° 57' Leo in an almost partile waxing semisextile aspect with natal Pluto at 22° 56' Cancer. By secondary progression, his Mercury, now at 7° 59' Sagittarius, was just separating from a waxing sesquiquadrate with natal Pluto. Transit Pluto was in the middle of forming seven conjunctions to progressed Mercury over a 32 month period. Mercury was the ruler of his 7th and 9th houses (Cancer intercepted in the 7th). He and his wife had separated the year before, and for the marriage to continue, its form had to change (progressed 7th ruler transited by Pluto). He was reconciling himself to that fact, and because he still loves his wife deeply, he was willing to try a new form of marriage for the first time in his life, one where they would live apart some of the time, and be together at other times. As the 9th house was also activated by this combination natal-progressed-transit episode, it was the return to his Catholic faith on a deeper level that was providing the inner spiritual strength to accept the changes.

The astrologer will find, when calculating transits to progressed planets or angles, some incessant occurrences such as a client receiving nine, 11, 13 or sometimes up to more than 25 exact aspects forming over a three to ten year period. This happens because *there is a moving target.* The all time record that I have ever seen in my practice was transit Pluto forming 53 squares to a client's secondary progressed Mercury over a 26 year period. Pluto, moving about 2.3° per year, and progressed Mercury, also moving a little over 2° per year, were setting up the same aspect to form again and again and again as transit Pluto went back and forth through its direct and retrograde degree movement, while progressed Mercury kept moving forward, thereby setting up more partile aspects. To quote the late Charles

E.O. Carter, whom I love and revere, as he had written in *The Zodiac and the Soul* regarding a 1953 eclipse, *"such an exceptional bombardment"* would certainly bring substantial change into the life of the client, both inner and outer, as this did.

Recently, in other client cases involving transits to progressions, I have seen the same aspect form 21 times over a 9 3/4 year period (transit Neptune square progressed ascendant), 13 times over a 68 month period (transit Pluto square secondary Mercury), or 9 times over a 46 month period (transit Pluto square progressed ascendant). In my view, the astrologer should pay more attention to these transits, which last so much longer and represent a gradual spiritual integration for the client, than to dwell on transits to natal planets that occur in a 10 to 20 month time period. While the client is going through the latter episode, he usually feels pretty helpless to do anything about it. At least with the transit-to-progressed episodes, the astrologer can *honestly and confidently* inform the client that he *will* integrate this experience, grow in spiritual character, and be the better for it. It is my experience that the progressed chart is more readily integrated into the higher self, while transits to the natal chart are often only endured and persevered through.

Table 14 - Progressions Consultation Preparation Checklist

A. Long-Term Cycles

1. Secondary progressed Sun-Moon phase
2. Saturn transit cycle phase
3. Jupiter transit cycle phase
4. Transit Saturn in house, hemisphere, quadrant
5. Transit Jupiter in house, hemisphere, quadrant
6. Secondary progressed Moon in natal house
7. Secondary progressed Moon in progressed house

B. Secondary Progressed Lunation Degrees & Sabian Symbols

1. Entry degree of current progressed Sun-Moon phase
2. Sabian symbol for this degree
3. Degree of previous progressed New Moon
4. Sabian symbol for this degree
5. Degree of previous progressed Full Moon
6. Sabian symbol for this degree
7. Degree of previous progressed Quarter Moon
8. Sabian symbol for this degree
9. New Moon Solar Eclipse?
10. Full Moon Lunar Eclipse?

C. Secondary Progressed Moon Aspects

1. Progressed Moon to natal aspects forming in next 6 months
2. Progressed Moon aspect matching natal Moon aspect?
3. Progressed Moon sign or house change?
4. Progressed Moon triggering progressed-to-natal?
5. Progressed Moon triggering transit-to-progressed?
6. Progressed Moon triggering transit-to-natal?
7. Progressed Moon approaching angularity?

D. Tertiary & Minor Progressed Moons

1. Tertiary progressed Sun-Moon phase
2. Minor progressed Sun-Moon phase
3. Most recent tertiary New or Full Moon degree
4. Sabian symbol for this degree
5. Most recent minor New or Full Moon degree
6. Sabian symbol for this degree
7. New Moon Solar Eclipse?
8. Full Moon Lunar Eclipse?
9. Matching degree with lifetime secondary lunations?

E. Secondary Progressed Sun

1. Progressed Sun sign & degree
2. Progressed Sun decanate
3. Progressed Sun dwad
4. Planetary subrulerships
5. Sabian symbol for this degree
6. Progressed Sun sign or house change?
7. Progressed Sun to natal aspects

F. Tertiary Progressed Sun

1. Tertiary Sun to natal Sun phase
2. Next phase change aspect
3. Tertiary Sun in natal house
4. Tertiary Sun sign or house change?
5. Tertiary Sun aspects to natal

G. Minor Progressed Sun

1. Minor Sun to natal Sun phase
2. Next phase change aspect
3. Minor Sun in natal house

    4. Minor Sun sign or house change?
    5. Minor Sun aspects to natal

H. Progressed Ascendant & Midheaven

    1. Current degrees of progressed horizon
    2. Sabian symbol for these degrees
    3. Current degrees of progressed meridian
    4. Sabian symbol for these degrees
    5. Progressed ascendant decanate
    6. Progressed ascendant dwad
    7. Planetary subrulerships
    8. Progressed midheaven decanate
    9. Progressed midheaven dwad
    10. Planetary subrulerships
    11. Progressed ascendant aspects to natal
    12. Progressed midheaven aspects to natal
    13. Progressed angle parans?

I. Secondary Progressed Mercury, Venus & Mars

    1. Secondary Mercury aspects to natal
    2. Secondary Venus aspects to natal
    3. Secondary Mars aspects to natal
    4. Any secondary retrogradation?
    5. Rx stationary date & degree
    6. Date & degree of direct station
    7. Triple aspects? Dates of 1st, 2nd, 3rd
    8. Stationary aspects? How long within 1° orb?
    9. Secondary sign changes?
    10. Secondary angularity?
    11. Secondary house changes?

J. Tertiary & Minor Progressed Mercury, Venus & Mars

    1. Any TP or MP retrogradation?
    2. Rx stationary date & degree
    3. Date & degree of direct station
    4. Triple aspects? Dates of 1st, 2nd, 3rd
    5. Stationary aspects? How long within 1° orb?
    6. TP or MP sign changes?
    7. TP or MP angularity?
    8. TP or MP house changes?
    9. TP Mercury to natal Mercury phase

      10. MP Mercury to natal Mercury phase
      11. TP Venus to natal Venus phase
      12. MP Venus to natal Venus phase
      13. TP Mars to natal Mars phase
      14. MP Mars to natal Mars phase

K. Secondary Progressed Jupiter & Saturn

      1. Secondary Jupiter aspects or stations?
      2. Secondary Saturn aspects or stations?
      3. Secondary Jupiter history
      4. Secondary Saturn history

L. Tertiary & Minor Progressed Jupiter & Saturn

      1. Tertiary Jupiter currently Rx or direct?
      2. Rx stationary date & degree
      3. Direct stationary date & degree
      4. Sabian symbol for these degrees
      5. Triple aspects? Dates of 1st, 2nd, 3rd
      6. Stationary aspects? How long within 1° orb?
      7. Minor Jupiter currently Rx or direct?
      8. Rx stationary date & degree
      9. Direct stationary date & degree
      10. Sabian symbol for these degrees
      11. Triple aspects? Dates of 1st, 2nd, 3rd
      12. Stationary aspects? How long within 1° orb?
      13. Tertiary Saturn currently Rx or direct?
      14. Rx stationary date & degree
      15. Direct stationary date & degree
      16. Sabian symbol for these degrees
      17. Triple aspects? Dates of 1st, 2nd, 3rd
      18. Stationary aspects? How long within 1° orb?
      19. Minor Saturn currently Rx or direct?
      20. Rx stationary date & degree
      21. Direct stationary date & degree
      22. Sabian symbol for these degrees
      23. Triple aspects? Dates of 1st, 2nd, 3rd
      24. Stationary aspects? How long within 1° orb?

M. Transits to Progressed Planets/Angles

      1. Transit Pluto to secondary planets/angles—duration & # of times
      2. Transit Neptune to secondary planets/angles—duration & # of times

3. Transit Uranus to secondary planets/angles—duration & # of times
4. Transit Saturn to secondary planets/angles—duration & # of times

N. Transits to Natal Planets/Angles

1. Transit Pluto conjunctions, oppositions or squares
2. Transit Neptune conjunctions, oppositions or squares
3. Transit Uranus conjunctions, oppositions or squares
4. Transit Saturn conjunctions, oppositions or squares

O. Progressed to Progressed Aspects

1. Secondary to secondary conjunctions
2. Secondary to secondary oppositions
3. Secondary to secondary squares
4. Tertiary to tertiary outer five planet conjunctions
5. Minor to minor outer five planet conjunctions
    (for 4. or 5. consider only Jupiter, Saturn, Uranus, Neptune or Pluto)

P. Natal to Progressed to Transit Links

1. Current secondary progressed to natal aspects between planets in a natal aspect relationship?
2. Sensitive degrees of these forming progressions
3. Dates of same two planets forming transit triggers to these degrees

Endnotes

1. The most infamous of the transit-to-progressed occurrence is transit Saturn in repeated aspect to a secondary progressed Moon. The Saturn transit cycle is 29.5 years in length, while the progressed Moon cycle is 27.3 years. Due to fluctuating motion of the Moon, and the elliptical nature of Saturn's orbit, the two will lock into a sequence of repeated aspects at some point in every life. The author became a full-time professional astrologer when transit Saturn formed the first of forty-three oppositions to his progressed Moon in August of 1989. As the rulers of his nodal axis, this has kept the pressure on him to succeed in self-employment despite any and all obstacles. The 43 oppositions will finally cease in February of 2011, after having lasted for over 21 years. One need not fear this phenomenon; rather one can dedicate themselves to achievement, accomplishment and service to others.

Chapter Eight
Miscellaneous Thoughts & Interpretive Strategies
Synastric Progressions

During the years I have worked with progressions, I have seen numerous partile (exact to the degree and minute) conjunctions between my natal or progressed chart and clients' natal or progressed birthcharts, calculated for the date of our appointment. After observing this phenomenon over and over again, I began to think about the significance of it. I would see a client, for example, whose secondary progressed Moon was at 6° 38' Pisces on the day of the consultation, the precise degree and minute of my natal Moon. Other clients would have progressed planets in a partile conjunction to the current degree and minute of my progressed Ascendant or Midheaven. Outside of my practice, I met a woman at the post office on the day her secondary progressed Venus was at 22° 44' Scorpio, in a partile conjunction to my natal Sun. She and I became very close friends.

Because of repeated episodes such as these, I began to view synastric progressions from a metaphysical perspective. It appeared as if a window of time, along with a degree link, was operating between the two birthcharts. The question of whether these progression links in synastry produce transitory versus permanent connections between people is still unanswered in my mind. I have seen it occur at the beginning of long-term relationships, as well as between myself and clients, which although our relationship may last for years, I only see them once or twice a year.

After this aroused my third house Mercury curiosity, I began to request the dates from clients of when they had first met their husband or wife. What I found, almost without exception, was an exact conjunction or opposition between one natal chart and one progressed chart, or between the two progressed charts. In many cases, the aspects were exact to both the degree and minute. My take on this phenomenon is that there are windows of opportunities for us throughout life and certain people arrive at these specific times, when the two birthcharts are linked by exact degrees.

The choice to connect or not connect is ours, of course, but the opportunity, I believe, is brought to us when the time is right. You can almost presume that during the month that your secondary progressed Moon is at 2° Scorpio, for example, several clients with natal planets in that degree will walk through the door. The only interpretive guidelines I can offer you to make sense of this occurrence would be to study the two planets linking by synastric progression, their house rulerships, and which planets they disposit. The specific nature of the relationship, I have found, can be understood in this manner.

The Progressed Composite Chart

Progressions can also be used to track a relationship as it moves through time. I have worked with several techniques for doing this, most notably transits to the composite chart or transits to the time-space relationship chart. The composite chart, which is derived from a near midpoint calculation of the two sets of natal planets and angles, does not exist in time nor space, and therefore, cannot be found in the ephemeris. On the other hand, the time-space chart, which is also referred to as the Davison chart, is calculated using the midpoints of the two natal latitudes and longitudes, as well as the date and time midway between the two birthdays. This chart does exist in time and space, and as such, one could presume that transits to it would be more reliable than to the artificially derived composite chart. However, my experience is exactly the opposite. I have found that transits to the composite chart activate change in a relationship when concurrent relational progressions occur.

To produce a progressed composite chart, you must first progress the two natal charts, and then produce a composite chart from the two progressed charts. I have used this technique with secondary, tertiary and minor progressions, and have found that the same levels of reality associated with the three different progression calculations in natal work equally apply to relationships. The changing mental dimension of a relationship can be seen through the minor progressed composite chart. The fluctuating emotional dimension of a relationship is found in the tertiary progressed composite chart. The physical and structural mutations that a relationship goes through are discovered in the secondary progressed composite chart.

Compared to progressed natal calculations, the planetary motion in the progressed composite charts is identical. For example, the secondary progressed composite Moon moves about one degree per month, and the secondary progressed composite Sun moves about one degree per year.

I will share with you a personal example from my life. When my ex-wife (who had a natal Sun-Uranus opposition) and I were living in Seattle in 1986, and both of us had been there for years, she abruptly announced one February day after returning from a vacation in Hawaii that she was going to move there. With or without me. Sure enough, in our secondary progressed composite chart (physical/structural changes), calculated for the day that we got on the plane, while our car was being loaded onto an ocean freighter, we had a partile conjunction of the Sun and Mercury at 21° 03' Capricorn, with both in a partile opposition with Uranus at 21° 03' Cancer in the progressed composite chart.

The secondary progressed composite Moon, late in the second decanate of Aries, was also moving into position to form a progressed cardinal grand cross, with progressed composite Neptune in Libra filling in the fourth corner. Needless to say, the remainder of the year was quite topsy-turvy for us, as we wound up living in Hawaii for only five months, then staying with a friend in Northern Idaho. Then I went on a road trip around the Western states for a month to seek the next place to live (settling on Napa, California), then we went to India, and finally, exhausted, got resettled again some seven months later. If you see a couple with approaching dynamic (0°-90°-180°) secondary progressed composite aspects *between planets in cardinal signs*, or *planets in angular houses*, you can almost be certain that the relationship will undergo some kind of structural change.

Progressed Time Twins

If one is born within three months of another person, the older individual's birth chart will eventually secondary progress into the younger individual's natal chart. Additionally, the younger individual's birth chart will converse progress into the older's. I have observed this phenomenon in my practice several times at the beginning of a personal relationship between two people very close in age. They met at the point in life where one natal chart was identical to the other progressed chart. In my mind this is especially karmic, and suggests a relationship that is reforming again across the lifetimes.

Converse Progressions

Progressed planets and angles can also be calculated going backwards in time from birth, using the very same rates of planetary motion as for forward progressions. Thus, in converse secondary progressed calculations, a 45 year-old would have secondary planetary positions 45 days *prior* to birth. I have not used converse progressions extensively enough to be able to write intelligently about them, but I will share with you my limited understanding of the technique.

I have seen converse progressions used to rectify birthcharts with an unknown or suspect time. After the astrologer is given eight or so important dates of significant life experience—marriage, birth of child, death of parent, serious illness or accident—the various techniques of rectification usually look for angular progressions or transits. If the same degree keeps showing up for each of these dates, in each of the different calculation methods, there is an excellent chance that it is the degree of either the ascendant or the midheaven.

Converse progression is one verifiable technique for *confirming the supreme importance of angularity* in astrology. Converse tertiary progressions, especially, seem to work accurately in rectification work. The newer astrology software programs on the market have streamlined this rectification process, as they are able to do several forward and backward progression calculations in a matter of minutes, saving hours and even days of work on what used to be an expensive and laborious process.

In my practice, I have observed the converse secondary progressed Moon being conjunct the natal 7th house ruler at the time of marriage. I have also seen the converse secondary progressed Sun conjunct Saturn at the time of marriage (this is only possible in birthcharts where the natal Sun is no more than 20-70 degrees ahead of the natal Saturn). At the birth of children, I have observed the converse tertiary progressed Moon conjunct Venus when it was a daughter, and conjunct Mars when it was a son. I have also seen the converse minor progressed North Node conjunct the natal Moon at the birth.

It is tempting for me to dive into some metaphysical or karmic speculation about why converse progressions produce such exact aspects on the dates of significant life experiences. But rather than tossing my two cents worth of opinion into the existing well of astrological knowledge, I will bow out gracefully and gladly refer the reader to Alan Leo's *The Progressed Horoscope*. He writes quite clearly about the rationale he saw behind converse progressions and directions, referring to the axial rotation of the earth, and the movement of chart angles into aspect with natal planets.

The End of Life Chart

From an ideal perspective, there is a progressed chart that represents the spiritual growth and integration that *can take place during the present life*. This chart is calculated for the third secondary progressed lunar return which occurs at age 81 years and some nine to ten months. This planetary picture, being the condition of the solar system 82 days after you were born, suggests to the esoteric astrologer the end purpose of life. This chart in no way or shape refers to a death date prediction, and the astrologer is duty-bound to only discuss it with the client in the abstract.

This end of life chart can be viewed as the missing second bookend on the shelf of life, complimenting the natal chart, and containing the spiritual aspirations to be attempted during this life. To calculate this chart, determine the exact date and time of the third secondary progressed Moon conjunction to the natal Moon. Then determine the derived date and time for the secondary progressions of that day. This derived date should be ± 82 days after your birth. Erect the chart using the natal latitude and longitude. This is also the third lunar return after birth. This chart can be interpreted as the spiritual goal of life.

I have the "Billy Graham" aspects in my end of life chart, which are a Sun-Venus conjunction trine to Jupiter. Eighty-two days after my birth brings me to February 5, 1954. The Aquarius Sun was conjunct Venus, and both in a waning trine to stationary direct Jupiter in Gemini. When I am feeling down, I remember this chart as the spiritual design of my life, and it reminds me to love others, be creative and to share knowledge freely. I can only hope that by the age of 82 I will be as sweet and loving as the Reverend Graham. If I weren't an astrologer, with that big ol' Jupiter on my Midheaven, I know that I would choose to be a preacher.

Metaphysical Time Vector Intersection

Because of the algebraic foundation of the three different progression calculations, wherein days, lunar months and years interchange between the three systems, a fascinating metaphysical time-twist occurs. If you determine the derived dates and times for a lifetime (81.96 years or three secondary lunar returns) of both tertiary and minor progressions, you will find that at the age of three you have completed a lifetime of tertiaries, and by the age of six and one and one half months you have completed a lifetime of minors. Then, *tertiary progress* the natal chart *to the end date of the minors*, and you arrive at the secondary progressed end of life chart derived date. Wait, there's more. *Minor progress* the natal chart *to the end date of the tertiaries*, and again you arrive at the secondary derived date of 82 days after birth.

This occurs because of the mathematical interplay inherent within the 1:13:27 mystic time ratio. A tertiary progressed Sun return happens every ± 27 years, 3.8 months, which is the yearly planetary motion in days for the minor progressions. A minor progressed Sun return occurs every ± 13 years, 4.4 months, which is the yearly planetary motion in days for the tertiary progressions.

The esoteric astrologer will delight in the contemplation of this time vector intersection. In my view, it implies that at a specific point in time, the three planes of consciousness all intersect in an epiphany of total spiritual harmony.

The Progressed Void-of-Course Moon

Those astrologers who work with the void Moon extensively, such as in horary or electional charting, may have pondered the correlation between real-time void Moon periods and progressed void Moon periods. It is common to see radically different lengths of time for the void Moon, depending on the current degrees of the other planets and the sign of the Moon.

A void-of-course Moon occurs between the time that the Moon forms her last Ptolemaic aspect (0°, 60°, 90°, 120° or 180°) in the present sign and enters the next sign. In real time, this can vary from a few minutes to over two days. Recently, Neptune was in the final degree of Capricorn just prior to re-entering Aquarius. When the Moon was in a sign that formed a Ptolemaic aspect to Capricorn, the final lunar aspect in that sign occurred at 29° and so many minutes. Therefore, the void period was quite short, as in some cases, it was under a half-hour until the

Moon entered the next sign.

We know that a quality of directionlessness accompanies void Moons, as well as poor decision making choices and incomplete outcomes. When you research the periods that a secondary progressed Moon goes void-of-course, you will find that they explain chapters of life where nothing was concluded, or a general aimlessness was experienced. Some void Moon periods last for over two days in real time, and this converts to *over two years in secondary progressed time*. The astrologer can help and comfort a client who is frustrated by the lack of accomplishment in his life, by informing him of the dates and duration of the progressed void Moon episode, and suggesting a strategy of patience and timing that concurs with the secondary Moon's entry into the next sign.

The Physical Reality

One of the core theses of my book is that reality operates on three different levels and simultaneously at three different rates of speed, and that the three different systems of progression calculations allow the astrologer to perceive at which level the client is experiencing any planetary influences. I have also introduced in this book holographic time link theory, which explains how childhood lunations and eclipses occurring in the tertiary or minor progressions are directly linked to the secondary lunations or eclipses occurring during adulthood. Now I must confess that I realize an astrologer such as myself, being predominantly a water-air mixture (thank you, God, for my Virgo ascendant), is operating at a much subtler and more ethereal level of perception than most astrologers with, say, several planets in earth signs. But within the family of progression calculations, there is something for everyone. If you are having a hard time either grasping some of the metaphysical concepts herein, or are of the mind that there is nothing verifiable about them, then by all means stick with the secondary progressions; you will get excellent results.

The most important thing to remember when working with secondary progressions is the physical link between the natal aspects and the progressed aspects. If your client has two planets in a natal aspect relationship and these same two planets are moving into a different aspect by secondary progression, this tells you immediately that it is a *priority progression*. When *those same two planets*, by transit, form eighth harmonic (0°, 45°, 90°, 135° or 180°) aspects to the progressed degrees, you can almost be certain that your client will experience the progression inwardly or outwardly in a most noticeable way. These transit trigger dates do not have to be used predictively by the astrologer, but in the case of certain progressed aspects, where some kind of danger or accident is possible, such as Mars square Pluto or Mars opposite Uranus, then I believe it is the astrologer's spiritual duty to warn the client to be extra careful on the days that the *same planets* would form a stressful transit aspect to the progressed degrees. There is a distinct difference between worrying a client and making a precautionary statement; the astrologer need only be careful in choosing words to accomplish this successfully.

Because secondary progressions so obviously correlate to life experience at the physical level, the astrologer can use them extensively to advise clients of health concerns and to recommend compensating strategies. If you do not have a medical astrology background, then you can still recommend that the client visit a naturopathic physician for a blood analysis if you find a health-related progression occurring. I have repeatedly seen, for example, secondary progressed Mars quincunx natal Neptune or Saturn result in an iron deficiency. This leads to depression because iron oxygenates the blood stream, and low iron equals less brain oxygen which equals loss of mental perspective.

The secondary progressed Sun moving into a stressful aspect with Saturn or Neptune will just about always fatigue the client, no matter what kind of shape or health he is in. Pregnant women will just about always have a difficult trimester when their secondary progressed Moon moves into difficult aspect with natal Mars or Saturn. The easiest childbirths take place when the mother's secondary progressed Moon sextiles or trines Jupiter at the time of birth.

The Emotional Reality

I am the first to admit that I do not always use tertiary progressions with all of my clients. If clients come to me for help in picking a time to expand their business, or for cosmetic surgery, I am not going to bring up their relationships with their mothers. However, a large percentage of my clientele have done a lot of spiritual and healing work and these clients are a pure joy to work with because I can enter into the subtle realms with them, using my watery astrological skills to define and describe the progressed activity that is affecting their emotional bodies on the desire plane. Most clients with some intellectual sophistication will appreciate astrological interpretations that span the range from Jungian theory to Eastern mysticism to heart-centered esoteric Christianity. Clients who are more simple and straightforward in their approach to life still need to talk about their feelings when they are struggling with painful circumstances. In both cases, the astrologer can employ tertiary progression calculations to help the client get a handle on any emotional turmoil they may be going through.

In the preventative medical model of the mind-body connection where physical problems are thought to be derived from previous unresolved emotional trauma, using tertiary progressions the skilled astrologer can identify stressful aspects, stations, retrogradation or lunations forming, and advise the client how to make conscious the feelings associated with the planetary activity. For example, I have a client who had the tertiary progressed Sun moving into an opposition with natal Pluto who began to have frightening dreams about her father. When I explained that these dreams were the residue of emotional impressions left over from youth, it became easier for the client to objectify what had previously been a troubling emotional episode by laughing at it using the therapeutic powers of humor and love.

Specific tertiary progressed aspects will always occur earlier in life than their secondary progressed counterparts, because of the 13:1 time ratio that exists between the two calculations. The time-links between the two are quite revealing and can offer insight. For example, if the client is experiencing a waxing square from the secondary progressed Sun to the natal Mars, the astrologer, by researching when this aspect occurred by tertiary progression earlier in life, can help the client immensely by precisely dating an earlier chapter of life that existed only on the desire plane, but now is coming into physical manifestation.

The Mental Reality

In my experience, only a small fraction of my clients can completely relate to their minor progressions. But what a praiseworthy group they are. The reason for this is because the minors are defining planetary influences operating on the mental plane, which is also known as the causative, or causal plane. At this level of reality, thought activity is sowing seeds for future emotional and physical reaping. An individual usually needs to have experienced several years of meditation practice or contemplative prayer to be able to have sufficiently developed the subtle perceptions of consciousness that would allow self-view at this level of complexity. The monitoring of personal thought is such an advanced level of spiritual practice that, realistically, the astrologer could not hope to use this progression technique with a majority of clients.

However, with those clients who are doing shamanic work with others, such as soul-retrieval, the astrologer can be a truly loving and protective asset in their lives by tracking their minor progressions with them. The work that these individuals do with others is extremely difficult as it involves contact with the spirit world which is fraught with all kinds of danger. As Jesus drove the demons out of the poor souls so afflicted in His day, so, too, in His name are some shamanic and angelic healers curing the spiritually diseased in modern times. These healers, for whom I have the utmost love and respect, seem to have emerged in recent times from the Chiron opposition Uranus extended aspect that began in the early 1950's. This is the signature for alternative healing if there ever was one.

Chiron was orbiting within a 5° orb of opposing Uranus from February 1951 until May 1990, some 39 years. This aspect was in effect at Chiron's discovery in 1977. We are only just now seeing the tip of the iceberg of alternative medicine and spiritual healing practitioners, which, in my view, will peak during the Neptune in Pisces era from April 2011 until January 2026. This prolonged aspect was possible because of the highly elliptical nature of Chiron's orbit, which spends less than two years in Libra, yet remains in Aries for over eight years. As such, Chiron travels between the seen and unseen worlds, within the orbit of Saturn at perihelion, and beyond the orbit of Uranus at aphelion. In this metaphor, Chiron can be equated with the Holy Spirit.

Bearing these particulars about Chiron in mind while recalling that minor progressions metaphysically correspond with Spirit entering Soul, as the lunar month for a year calculations represent the Moon-Sun relationship, the astrologer can help these healers by informing them when they need to take a temporary sabbatical from their work, or by informing them when they can let it rip and do all the soul retrieval and spirit depossesion work they can possibly schedule. This is accomplished by the astrologer's proper interpretation of their minor progressed aspects, lunations, eclipses, retrogradation, stations and planetary returns.

Difficult planetary activity occurring in the minor progressions can result in spiritual warfare in the heavenly realms within which these healers are moving about. The minor progressions reveal the subtle activity taking place on the mental plane where all electrical healing (Chiron-Uranus) takes place. If the astrologer is getting into deep water by attempting spiritual interpretations beyond his experience and skill level, not to mention his level of spiritual protection, hopefully he will have the good sense to decline the work until he has had sufficient training to undertake this level of astrological subtlety.

Planetary Contact Between Planes of Consciousness

The most difficult progressed aspects to interpret, while at the same time the most fascinating, are the minor to tertiary, minor to secondary, and tertiary to secondary aspects. This planetary contact is occurring between different levels of consciousness as opposed to the holographic time links that include aspects, lunations, eclipses and stations *that predate one another*. This interplay of the mental plane, emotional plane and physical plane of planetary activity is of the utmost importance to esoteric astrologers as it can inform them how seed thoughts or feelings make their way down into concrete, physical manifestation. There are times when clients reach spiritual alignment with their higher selves and aspects such as minor Sun trine secondary Sun or tertiary ascendant ruler trine secondary ascendant ruler inform the esoteric astrologer when this is taking place.

The progressed planetary returns, such as the minor progressed Sun completing a cycle every 13 1/3 years, or the tertiary Sun completing a cycle every

27 1/3 years and returning to a conjunction with the natal Sun, can also be calculated between the different systems of progression. In this case, the astrologer would look at when the minor or tertiary Sun was conjunct the secondary Sun, with the difference being similar to sidereal versus synodic lunations.

If any of my readers are so inclined, I would recommend the following research to you. Because the minor progressions are moving in a 27:13 time ratio compared to the tertiaries, there will be same-planet conjunctions that take place between these two planes of consciousness (mental-emotional). For example, you know that Mars has an approximate two year orbital cycle in real time. In multidimensional progression work, this informs you that when the derived date of your client's minor progressions is about two years ahead of the derived date of their tertiary progressions, there will be a minor Mars conjunction to the tertiary Mars. I have found these interplane conjunctions between the Sun, Moon, Mercury, Venus and Mars to be highly significant in the process of spiritual integration. The mental and emotional bodies in alignment can produce feelings of spiritual unity that are tangibly blissful. When this planetary alignment is brought to the client's attention, a subtle union between the thoughts and feelings takes place. In like manner, when there are same-planet conjunctions between the minor and secondary, or tertiary and secondary progressions, the client is undergoing either a mental-physical plane, or an emotional-physical plane alignment.

The Consultation Preparation "Short List"

Some of my readers, after going through the progressions consultation preparation checklist at the end of Chapter Seven, may have despaired at the thought of so much work to prepare for the appointment with your client. Ideally, the professional consulting astrologer would be able to schedule a series of three to five appointments of ninety-minutes each to adequately and thoroughly interpret the whole scenario of progressed activity for any given client. However, as this is not an ideal world, most of my clients schedule one ninety-minute appointment every six months or year. In this limited time, my clients expect me to provide them with a concise summary of the *most important* progressed activity taking place.

I would recommend to practicing astrologers the following consultation content. I have used this system for years and, based on my professional experience, it consistently brings up the most relevant planetary activity.

    1. Current secondary progressed Sun-Moon phase
    2. Sabian symbol for entry degree of this phase; duration of phase
    3. Past date and Sabian symbol of current lunation cycle New Moon
    4. If waning, date and Sabian symbol of current cycle Full Moon

5. Secondary Moon in which natal house; check for angularity
6. Secondary Moon in which progressed house; check for angularity
7. Secondary Moon conjunctions or oppositions to natal planets in the next six months; emphasis on natal aspect planetary pairs, and trigger degrees to transit-progressed or progressed-natal aspects
8. Secondary Sun aspects (any and all) to natal planets or angles
9. Secondary Sun sign, decanate, dwad, current degree & Sabian symbol
10. Any secondary Sun sign ingress, angularity or house ingress
11. Secondary ascendant or midheaven aspects to natal (conjunction, opposition, square or quincunx only)
12. Current degree, Sabian symbol, sign decanate & dwad of progressed ascendant and MC (note planetary subrulerships)
13. Secondary Mercury, Venus or Mars aspects to natal planets/angles; check for sign ingresses, angularity, house ingresses
14. Any secondary Mercury, Venus or Mars retrogradation, stationary dates and degrees, triple aspects or stationary aspects
15. Secondary Jupiter and Saturn history: stations, conjunctions to natal
16. Transit Pluto, Neptune, Uranus or Saturn to *secondary progressed planets/angles* (conjunction, opposition, square, quincunx only)
17. Transit Pluto, Neptune, Uranus, Saturn or Jupiter conjunctions, oppositions or squares to natal planets/angles
18. Transit Mars, Jupiter & Saturn cycles (planet cycle & house cycle)
19. Lunations or eclipses falling on progressed "sensitive degrees"
20. Solar return planets in conjunction with natal or progressed planets

I can assure you that by following these consultation preparation guidelines, you will consistently relate to your client's current life experiences. This system of preparation, after some experience, should take about an hour and a half to research after calculating your charts.

Final Thoughts

It is my sincere hope and prayer that this book will help you to help your clients gain perspective on the life changes that they are going through by using progressions in your consultation work. It is for you, the practicing astrologer, that this book was written. I know what it takes, year in and year out to maintain a practice of astrology. The required spiritual effort prior to an appointment, so that you may love and serve your client, is very difficult to make at times. I send each of you my love, admiration and respect for the good work that you are doing in a world that does not always honor our profession. Please keep the faith because the work you are doing is truly worthwhile and you should be proud of yourself for having made the commitment to become a professional astrologer. God bless you, my friend.

Appendix I

These tables were calculated using Solar Fire for Windows, v. 4.12 © 1994-1998 Esoteric Technologies Pty. Ltd.
Time given is PDT (7 hours west of Greenwich)

Table 15 - Planet Stations 1920-2010

Mer	Retrograde	Mar 10 1920	13:44	04° Ar 41' R
Mar	Retrograde	Mar 14 1920	19:57	09° Sc 06' R
Mer	Direct	Apr 2 1920	15:33	21° Pi 39' D
Jup	Direct	Apr 3 1920	17:41	08° Le 06' D
Sat	Direct	May 6 1920	16:01	04° Vi 49' D
Mar	Direct	May 31 1920	15:19	21° Li 15' D
Mer	Retrograde	Jul 13 1920	06:58	10° Le 18' R
Mer	Direct	Aug 6 1920	10:30	29° Cn 15' D
Mer	Retrograde	Nov 5 1920	05:40	02° Sg 11' R
Mer	Direct	Nov 25 1920	05:43	16° Sc 06' D
Jup	Retrograde	Jan 3 1921	13:51	18° Vi 55' R
Sat	Retrograde	Jan 4 1921	02:26	24° Vi 48' R
Mer	Retrograde	Feb 21 1921	16:05	17° Pi 45' R
Mer	Direct	Mar 16 1921	01:49	03° Pi 29' D
Ven	Retrograde	Apr 1 1921	04:15	10° Ta 16' R
Jup	Direct	May 5 1921	17:57	08° Vi 56' D
Ven	Direct	May 13 1921	17:23	23° Ar 52' D
Sat	Direct	May 20 1921	13:25	17° Vi 58' D
Mer	Retrograde	Jun 24 1921	17:21	20° Cn 51' R
Mer	Direct	Jul 18 1921	22:27	11° Cn 10' D
Mer	Retrograde	Oct 19 1921	16:53	16° Sc 17' R
Mer	Direct	Nov 9 1921	04:10	00° Sc 26' D
Sat	Retrograde	Jan 16 1922	21:53	07° Li 36' R
Jup	Retrograde	Feb 2 1922	15:58	18° Li 54' R
Mer	Retrograde	Feb 5 1922	04:28	01° Pi 13' R
Mer	Direct	Feb 26 1922	20:05	16° Aq 03' D
Mar	Retrograde	May 7 1922	23:10	25° Sg 16' R
Sat	Direct	Jun 3 1922	04:34	00° Li 49' D
Mer	Retrograde	Jun 5 1922	15:32	00° Cn 53' R
Jup	Direct	Jun 5 1922	21:05	08° Li 58' D
Mer	Direct	Jun 29 1922	16:21	22° Ge 08' D
Mar	Direct	Jul 16 1922	19:06	11° Sg 06' D
Mer	Retrograde	Oct 2 1922	23:10	00° Sc 11' R
Mer	Direct	Oct 24 1922	02:10	14° Li 41' D

Ven	Retrograde	Nov 4 1922	08:18	09° Sg 50' R
Ven	Direct	Dec 15 1922	10:04	24° Sc 30' D
Mer	Retrograde	Jan 19 1923	22:51	14° Aq 58' R
Sat	Retrograde	Jan 29 1923	10:08	20° Li 07' R
Mer	Direct	Feb 9 1923	21:13	29° Cp 12' D
Jup	Retrograde	Mar 5 1923	11:23	18° Sc 56' R
Mer	Retrograde	May 17 1923	05:25	10° Ge 53' R
Mer	Direct	Jun 10 1923	02:04	02° Ge 18' D
Sat	Direct	Jun 16 1923	13:44	13° Li 21' D
Jup	Direct	Jul 7 1923	00:34	09° Sc 04' D
Mer	Retrograde	Sep 16 1923	00:03	13° Li 47' R
Mer	Direct	Oct 7 1923	21:40	28° Vi 49' D
Mer	Retrograde	Jan 3 1924	20:07	28° Cp 56' R
Mer	Direct	Jan 24 1924	04:17	12° Cp 49' D
Sat	Retrograde	Feb 10 1924	17:16	02° Sc 20' R
Jup	Retrograde	Apr 5 1924	17:59	19° Sg 54' R
Mer	Retrograde	Apr 26 1924	21:22	21° Ta 22' R
Mer	Direct	May 20 1924	17:15	12° Ta 04' D
Ven	Retrograde	Jun 9 1924	17:47	17° Cn 35' R
Sat	Direct	Jun 28 1924	16:36	25° Li 37' D
Ven	Direct	Jul 22 1924	20:29	01° Cn 03' D
Mar	Retrograde	Jul 24 1924	04:02	05° Pi 19' R
Jup	Direct	Aug 6 1924	18:21	10° Sg 03' D
Mer	Retrograde	Aug 28 1924	18:43	26° Vi 55' R
Mer	Direct	Sep 20 1924	11:56	12° Vi 42' D
Mar	Direct	Sep 22 1924	02:10	25° Aq 20' D
Mer	Retrograde	Dec 17 1924	17:53	13° Cp 02' R
Mer	Direct	Jan 6 1925	16:20	26° Sg 46' D
Sat	Retrograde	Feb 21 1925	20:39	14° Sc 19' R
Mer	Retrograde	Apr 8 1925	03:57	02° Ta 39' R
Mer	Direct	May 1 1925	21:08	22° Ar 01' D
Jup	Retrograde	May 10 1925	07:36	22° Cp 31' R
Sat	Direct	Jul 11 1925	12:40	07° Sc 38' D
Mer	Retrograde	Aug 11 1925	06:21	09° Vi 27' R
Mer	Direct	Sep 3 1925	17:26	26° Le 18' D
Jup	Direct	Sep 8 1925	23:38	12° Cp 41' D
Mer	Retrograde	Dec 1 1925	14:22	27° Sg 12' R
Mer	Direct	Dec 21 1925	08:36	10° Sg 55' D
Ven	Retrograde	Jan 17 1926	15:08	26° Aq 04' R
Ven	Direct	Feb 27 1926	21:43	10° Aq 20' D
Sat	Retrograde	Mar 5 1926	20:37	26° Sc 05' R

Mer	Retrograde	Mar 21 1926	05:48	14° Ar 45' R
Mer	Direct	Apr 13 1926	14:29	02° Ar 34' D
Jup	Retrograde	Jun 16 1926	00:58	27° Aq 10' R
Sat	Direct	Jul 24 1926	01:52	19° Sc 25' D
Mer	Retrograde	Jul 24 1926	09:59	21° Le 14' R
Mer	Direct	Aug 17 1926	09:48	09° Le 23' D
Mar	Retrograde	Sep 28 1926	22:38	19° Ta 28' R
Jup	Direct	Oct 13 1926	21:18	17° Aq 19' D
Mer	Retrograde	Nov 15 1926	08:11	11° Sg 23' R
Mer	Direct	Dec 5 1926	04:16	25° Sc 12' D
Mar	Direct	Dec 6 1926	19:25	04° Ta 32' D
Mer	Retrograde	Mar 4 1927	00:27	27° Pi 30' R
Sat	Retrograde	Mar 17 1927	17:02	07° Sg 40' R
Mer	Direct	Mar 26 1927	19:27	13° Pi 55' D
Mer	Retrograde	Jul 6 1927	03:44	02° Le 13' R
Jup	Retrograde	Jul 24 1927	05:20	03° Ar 31' R
Mer	Direct	Jul 30 1927	08:35	21° Cn 46' D
Sat	Direct	Aug 5 1927	10:29	01° Sg 01' D
Ven	Retrograde	Aug 20 1927	04:38	24° Vi 59' R
Ven	Direct	Oct 1 1927	19:47	08° Vi 51' D
Mer	Retrograde	Oct 29 1927	22:12	25° Sc 32' R
Mer	Direct	Nov 19 1927	02:09	09° Sc 32' D
Jup	Direct	Nov 19 1927	11:01	23° Pi 37' D
Mer	Retrograde	Feb 15 1928	07:28	10° Pi 46' R
Mer	Direct	Mar 8 1928	09:37	26° Aq 04' D
Sat	Retrograde	Mar 28 1928	11:56	19° Sg 08' R
Mer	Retrograde	Jun 16 1928	09:04	12° Cn 30' R
Mer	Direct	Jul 10 1928	12:15	03° Cn 16' D
Sat	Direct	Aug 16 1928	15:33	12° Sg 30' D
Jup	Retrograde	Aug 30 1928	01:47	10° Ta 25' R
Mer	Retrograde	Oct 12 1928	07:25	09° Sc 33' R
Mer	Direct	Nov 2 1928	00:45	23° Li 50' D
Mar	Retrograde	Nov 11 1928	21:07	09° Cn 17' R
Jup	Direct	Dec 25 1928	13:20	00° Ta 26' D
Mar	Direct	Jan 27 1929	04:54	20° Ge 59' D
Mer	Retrograde	Jan 28 1929	22:41	24° Aq 22' R
Mer	Direct	Feb 19 1929	07:01	08° Aq 54' D
Ven	Retrograde	Mar 29 1929	19:59	08° Ta 03' R
Sat	Retrograde	Apr 9 1929	08:12	00° Cp 31' R
Ven	Direct	May 11 1929	07:58	21° Ar 39' D
Mer	Retrograde	May 28 1929	02:11	22° Ge 26' R

Mer	Direct	Jun 21 1929	01:23	13° Ge 53' D
Sat	Direct	Aug 28 1929	17:05	23° Sg 54' D
Mer	Retrograde	Sep 25 1929	11:16	23° Li 22' R
Jup	Retrograde	Oct 5 1929	02:24	16° Ge 24' R
Mer	Direct	Oct 16 1929	22:08	08° Li 03' D
Mer	Retrograde	Jan 12 1930	18:38	08° Aq 14' R
Jup	Direct	Jan 31 1930	01:35	06° Ge 21' D
Mer	Direct	Feb 2 1930	10:36	22° Cp 17' D
Sat	Retrograde	Apr 21 1930	06:08	11° Cp 53' R
Mer	Retrograde	May 8 1930	15:14	02° Ge 35' R
Mer	Direct	Jun 1 1930	11:32	23° Ta 48' D
Mer	Retrograde	Sep 8 1930	09:26	06° Li 47' R
Sat	Direct	Sep 9 1930	14:58	05° Cp 15' D
Mer	Direct	Sep 30 1930	15:46	22° Vi 06' D
Ven	Retrograde	Nov 1 1930	20:47	07° Sg 23' R
Jup	Retrograde	Nov 7 1930	19:29	20° Cn 31' R
Ven	Direct	Dec 12 1930	23:19	22° Sc 02' D
Mar	Retrograde	Dec 18 1930	06:32	16° Le 49' R
Mer	Retrograde	Dec 27 1930	16:31	22° Cp 16' R
Mer	Direct	Jan 16 1931	19:45	06° Cp 04' D
Jup	Direct	Mar 7 1931	00:48	10° Cn 27' D
Mar	Direct	Mar 8 1931	06:42	27° Cn 26' D
Mer	Retrograde	Apr 19 1931	12:46	13° Ta 24' R
Sat	Retrograde	May 3 1931	05:44	23° Cp 17' R
Mer	Direct	May 13 1931	07:26	03° Ta 35' D
Mer	Retrograde	Aug 22 1931	01:26	19° Vi 41' R
Mer	Direct	Sep 14 1931	02:36	05° Vi 54' D
Sat	Direct	Sep 21 1931	11:34	16° Cp 39' D
Jup	Retrograde	Dec 9 1931	09:24	22° Le 38' R
Mer	Retrograde	Dec 11 1931	14:03	06° Cp 24' R
Mer	Direct	Dec 31 1931	09:47	20° Sg 06' D
Mer	Retrograde	Mar 31 1932	03:20	25° Ar 02' R
Jup	Direct	Apr 8 1932	06:25	12° Le 36' D
Mer	Direct	Apr 23 1932	17:40	13° Ar 45' D
Sat	Retrograde	May 14 1932	08:41	04° Aq 46' R
Ven	Retrograde	Jun 7 1932	10:32	15° Cn 26' R
Ven	Direct	Jul 20 1932	13:18	28° Ge 55' D
Mer	Retrograde	Aug 3 1932	10:07	01° Vi 54' R
Mer	Direct	Aug 27 1932	02:56	19° Le 17' D
Sat	Direct	Oct 2 1932	09:18	28° Cp 07' D
Mer	Retrograde	Nov 24 1932	09:32	20° Sg 35' R

Mer	Direct	Dec 14 1932	03:48	04° Sg 20' D
Jup	Retrograde	Jan 7 1933	18:26	23° Vi 16' R
Mar	Retrograde	Jan 20 1933	18:16	20° Vi 17' R
Mer	Retrograde	Mar 13 1933	12:37	07° Ar 27' R
Mer	Direct	Apr 5 1933	16:29	24° Pi 38' D
Mar	Direct	Apr 11 1933	19:09	00° Vi 52' D
Jup	Direct	May 10 1933	02:54	13° Vi 17' D
Sat	Retrograde	May 26 1933	17:29	16° Aq 23' R
Mer	Retrograde	Jul 16 1933	09:30	13° Le 20' R
Mer	Direct	Aug 9 1933	12:25	02° Le 04' D
Sat	Direct	Oct 14 1933	08:37	09° Aq 43' D
Mer	Retrograde	Nov 8 1933	01:40	04° Sg 45' R
Mer	Direct	Nov 28 1933	00:34	18° Sc 39' D
Ven	Retrograde	Jan 15 1934	04:40	23° Aq 38' R
Jup	Retrograde	Feb 6 1934	22:33	23° Li 12' R
Mer	Retrograde	Feb 24 1934	13:10	20° Pi 27' R
Ven	Direct	Feb 25 1934	10:39	07° Aq 57' D
Mer	Direct	Mar 19 1934	01:19	06° Pi 21' D
Sat	Retrograde	Jun 8 1934	08:40	28° Aq 11' R
Jup	Direct	Jun 10 1934	06:13	13° Li 16' D
Mer	Retrograde	Jun 27 1934	21:51	23° Cn 59' R
Mer	Direct	Jul 22 1934	03:15	14° Cn 08' D
Mer	Retrograde	Oct 22 1934	13:37	18° Sc 53' R
Sat	Direct	Oct 26 1934	09:19	21° Aq 30' D
Mer	Direct	Nov 11 1934	22:51	02° Sc 58' D
Mer	Retrograde	Feb 8 1935	00:18	03° Pi 51' R
Mar	Retrograde	Feb 27 1935	05:00	24° Li 37' R
Mer	Direct	Mar 1 1935	18:30	18° Aq 48' D
Jup	Retrograde	Mar 9 1935	19:03	23° Sc 18' R
Mar	Direct	May 17 1935	14:32	06° Li 03' D
Mer	Retrograde	Jun 8 1935	22:00	04° Cn 05' R
Sat	Retrograde	Jun 21 1935	06:16	10° Pi 13' R
Mer	Direct	Jul 2 1935	23:18	25° Ge 14' D
Jup	Direct	Jul 11 1935	08:08	13° Sc 25' D
Ven	Retrograde	Aug 17 1935	18:39	22° Vi 46' R
Ven	Direct	Sep 29 1935	10:42	06° Vi 36' D
Mer	Retrograde	Oct 5 1935	20:46	02° Sc 48' R
Mer	Direct	Oct 26 1935	21:03	17° Li 14' D
Sat	Direct	Nov 7 1935	13:19	03° Pi 30' D
Mer	Retrograde	Jan 22 1936	17:58	17° Aq 35' R
Mer	Direct	Feb 12 1936	18:50	01° Aq 53' D

Jup	Retrograde	Apr 10 1936	10:06	24° Sg 26' R
Mer	Retrograde	May 19 1936	12:20	14° Ge 03' R
Mer	Direct	Jun 12 1936	09:29	05° Ge 30' D
Sat	Retrograde	Jul 3 1936	10:00	22° Pi 32' R
Jup	Direct	Aug 11 1936	07:33	14° Sg 35' D
Mer	Retrograde	Sep 17 1936	22:26	16° Li 27' R
Mer	Direct	Oct 9 1936	17:10	01° Li 23' D
Sat	Direct	Nov 18 1936	23:05	15° Pi 47' D
Mer	Retrograde	Jan 5 1937	14:56	01° Aq 32' R
Mer	Direct	Jan 26 1937	01:04	15° Cp 27' D
Ven	Retrograde	Mar 27 1937	12:04	05° Ta 50' R
Mar	Retrograde	Apr 14 1937	07:33	05° Sg 32' R
Mer	Retrograde	Apr 30 1937	02:57	24° Ta 26' R
Ven	Direct	May 8 1937	22:52	19° Ar 27' D
Jup	Retrograde	May 15 1937	05:18	27° Cp 19' R
Mer	Direct	May 23 1937	23:10	15° Ta 18' D
Mar	Direct	Jun 27 1937	03:03	19° Sc 32' D
Sat	Retrograde	Jul 16 1937	20:56	05° Ar 08' R
Mer	Retrograde	Aug 31 1937	18:01	29° Vi 41' R
Jup	Direct	Sep 13 1937	15:43	17° Cp 29' D
Mer	Direct	Sep 23 1937	08:31	15° Vi 21' D
Sat	Direct	Dec 1 1937	15:01	28° Pi 21' D
Mer	Retrograde	Dec 20 1937	12:47	15° Cp 37' R
Mer	Direct	Jan 9 1938	12:22	29° Sg 21' D
Mer	Retrograde	Apr 11 1938	07:06	05° Ta 36' R
Mer	Direct	May 5 1938	00:48	25° Ar 11' D
Jup	Retrograde	Jun 21 1938	07:59	02° Pi 15' R
Sat	Retrograde	Jul 30 1938	15:20	18° Ar 03' R
Mer	Retrograde	Aug 14 1938	06:45	12° Vi 19' R
Mer	Direct	Sep 6 1938	15:32	28° Le 59' D
Jup	Direct	Oct 18 1938	21:56	22° Aq 24' D
Ven	Retrograde	Oct 30 1938	09:19	04° Sg 56' R
Mer	Retrograde	Dec 4 1938	09:38	29° Sg 46' R
Ven	Direct	Dec 10 1938	12:51	19° Sc 34' D
Sat	Direct	Dec 14 1938	13:07	11° Ar 14' D
Mer	Direct	Dec 24 1938	04:02	13° Sg 29' D
Mer	Retrograde	Mar 24 1939	06:11	17° Ar 34' R
Mer	Direct	Apr 16 1939	16:19	05° Ar 37' D
Mar	Retrograde	Jun 22 1939	11:30	04° Aq 42' R
Mer	Retrograde	Jul 27 1939	11:48	24° Le 13' R
Jup	Retrograde	Jul 29 1939	13:19	08° Ar 48' R

Sat	Retrograde	Aug 13 1939	16:41	01° Ta 16' R
Mer	Direct	Aug 20 1939	10:01	12° Le 09' D
Mar	Direct	Aug 23 1939	16:53	23° Cp 55' D
Mer	Retrograde	Nov 18 1939	03:57	13° Sg 57' R
Jup	Direct	Nov 24 1939	13:39	28° Pi 52' D
Mer	Direct	Dec 7 1939	23:16	27° Sc 45' D
Sat	Direct	Dec 27 1939	17:19	24° Ar 25' D
Mer	Retrograde	Mar 5 1940	22:25	00° Ar 14' R
Mer	Direct	Mar 28 1940	19:51	16° Pi 51' D
Ven	Retrograde	Jun 5 1940	03:01	13° Cn 18' R
Mer	Retrograde	Jul 8 1940	07:11	05° Le 18' R
Ven	Direct	Jul 18 1940	06:10	26° Ge 47' D
Mer	Direct	Aug 1 1940	11:36	24° Cn 38' D
Sat	Retrograde	Aug 26 1940	23:22	14° Ta 47' R
Jup	Retrograde	Sep 4 1940	05:36	15° Ta 41' R
Mer	Retrograde	Oct 31 1940	18:32	28° Sc 06' R
Mer	Direct	Nov 20 1940	20:57	12° Sc 04' D
Jup	Direct	Dec 30 1940	17:48	05° Ta 41' D
Sat	Direct	Jan 9 1941	04:19	07° Ta 54' D
Mer	Retrograde	Feb 17 1941	03:50	13° Pi 26' R
Mer	Direct	Mar 11 1941	08:46	28° Aq 53' D
Mer	Retrograde	Jun 19 1941	14:11	15° Cn 40' R
Mer	Direct	Jul 13 1941	18:09	06° Cn 17' D
Mar	Retrograde	Sep 6 1941	11:34	23° Ar 43' R
Sat	Retrograde	Sep 10 1941	09:42	28° Ta 33' R
Jup	Retrograde	Oct 10 1941	00:23	21° Ge 27' R
Mer	Retrograde	Oct 15 1941	04:23	12° Sc 09' R
Mer	Direct	Nov 4 1941	19:33	26° Li 23' D
Mar	Direct	Nov 10 1941	01:29	11° Ar 04' D
Ven	Retrograde	Jan 12 1942	17:38	21° Aq 11' R
Sat	Direct	Jan 22 1942	22:35	21° Ta 38' D
Mer	Retrograde	Jan 31 1942	18:08	27° Aq 00' R
Jup	Direct	Feb 5 1942	02:10	11° Ge 23' D
Mer	Direct	Feb 22 1942	05:01	11° Aq 38' D
Ven	Direct	Feb 22 1942	22:57	05° Aq 32' D
Mer	Retrograde	May 31 1942	08:56	25° Ge 38' R
Mer	Direct	Jun 24 1942	08:48	17° Ge 01' D
Sat	Retrograde	Sep 24 1942	21:57	12° Ge 31' R
Mer	Retrograde	Sep 28 1942	09:06	26° Li 00' R
Mer	Direct	Oct 19 1942	17:14	10° Li 37' D
Jup	Retrograde	Nov 12 1942	06:33	25° Cn 14' R

Mer	Retrograde	Jan 15 1943	13:39	10° Aq 50' R
Mer	Direct	Feb 5 1943	07:43	24° Cp 56' D
Sat	Direct	Feb 5 1943	23:27	05° Ge 35' D
Jup	Direct	Mar 11 1943	18:29	15° Cn 10' D
Mer	Retrograde	May 11 1943	22:07	05° Ge 43' R
Mer	Direct	Jun 4 1943	18:24	27° Ta 01' D
Ven	Retrograde	Aug 15 1943	09:34	20° Vi 33' R
Mer	Retrograde	Sep 11 1943	08:16	09° Li 29' R
Ven	Direct	Sep 27 1943	02:11	04° Vi 21' D
Mer	Direct	Oct 3 1943	11:34	24° Vi 41' D
Sat	Retrograde	Oct 9 1943	10:16	26° Ge 38' R
Mar	Retrograde	Oct 27 1943	22:12	22° Ge 14' R
Jup	Retrograde	Dec 13 1943	15:31	27° Le 04' R
Mer	Retrograde	Dec 30 1943	11:25	24° Cp 51' R
Mar	Direct	Jan 9 1944	21:33	04° Ge 51' D
Mer	Direct	Jan 19 1944	16:13	08° Cp 39' D
Sat	Direct	Feb 20 1944	05:23	19° Ge 41' D
Jup	Direct	Apr 12 1944	18:34	17° Le 02' D
Mer	Retrograde	Apr 21 1944	17:28	16° Ta 24' R
Mer	Direct	May 15 1944	12:34	06° Ta 47' D
Mer	Retrograde	Aug 24 1944	01:19	22° Vi 28' R
Mer	Direct	Sep 15 1944	23:39	08° Vi 32' D
Sat	Retrograde	Oct 22 1944	21:08	10° Cn 47' R
Mer	Retrograde	Dec 13 1944	09:03	08° Cp 57' R
Mer	Direct	Jan 2 1945	05:38	22° Sg 40' D
Jup	Retrograde	Jan 11 1945	20:54	27° Vi 30' R
Sat	Direct	Mar 5 1945	14:26	03° Cn 50' D
Ven	Retrograde	Mar 25 1945	04:21	03° Ta 35' R
Mer	Retrograde	Apr 3 1945	05:05	27° Ar 55' R
Mer	Direct	Apr 26 1945	20:40	16° Ar 52' D
Ven	Direct	May 6 1945	13:58	17° Ar 12' D
Jup	Direct	May 14 1945	10:03	17° Vi 31' D
Mer	Retrograde	Aug 6 1945	11:04	04° Vi 48' R
Mer	Direct	Aug 30 1945	01:55	21° Le 59' D
Sat	Retrograde	Nov 6 1945	04:44	24° Cn 54' R
Mer	Retrograde	Nov 27 1945	04:53	23° Sg 07' R
Mar	Retrograde	Dec 4 1945	15:38	03° Le 14' R
Mer	Direct	Dec 16 1945	23:04	06° Sg 53' D
Jup	Retrograde	Feb 11 1946	00:31	27° Li 22' R
Mar	Direct	Feb 21 1946	14:01	14° Cn 06' D
Mer	Retrograde	Mar 16 1946	11:49	10° Ar 13' R

Sat	Direct	Mar 20 1946	00:50	17° Cn 57' D
Mer	Direct	Apr 8 1946	17:32	27° Pi 38' D
Jup	Direct	Jun 14 1946	10:39	17° Li 27' D
Mer	Retrograde	Jul 19 1946	11:49	16° Le 21' R
Mer	Direct	Aug 12 1946	13:57	04° Le 53' D
Ven	Retrograde	Oct 27 1946	21:48	02° Sg 29' R
Mer	Retrograde	Nov 10 1946	21:36	07° Sg 18' R
Sat	Retrograde	Nov 20 1946	07:21	08° Le 53' R
Mer	Direct	Nov 30 1946	19:25	21° Sc 10' D
Ven	Direct	Dec 8 1946	02:30	17° Sc 07' D
Mer	Retrograde	Feb 27 1947	10:28	23° Pi 09' R
Jup	Retrograde	Mar 14 1947	03:50	27° Sc 34' R
Mer	Direct	Mar 22 1947	00:59	09° Pi 13' D
Sat	Direct	Apr 3 1947	10:54	01° Le 57' D
Mer	Retrograde	Jul 1 1947	02:06	27° Cn 07' R
Jup	Direct	Jul 15 1947	15:36	17° Sc 42' D
Mer	Direct	Jul 25 1947	07:31	17° Cn 03' D
Mer	Retrograde	Oct 25 1947	10:18	21° Sc 26' R
Mer	Direct	Nov 14 1947	17:33	05° Sc 29' D
Sat	Retrograde	Dec 4 1947	03:23	22° Le 41' R
Mar	Retrograde	Jan 8 1948	06:39	07° Vi 37' R
Mer	Retrograde	Feb 10 1948	20:17	06° Pi 30' R
Mer	Direct	Mar 3 1948	17:12	21° Aq 33' D
Mar	Direct	Mar 29 1948	05:27	18° Le 06' D
Jup	Retrograde	Apr 15 1948	00:39	28° Sg 56' R
Sat	Direct	Apr 16 1948	19:21	15° Le 45' D
Ven	Retrograde	Jun 2 1948	18:58	11° Cn 09' R
Mer	Retrograde	Jun 11 1948	04:09	07° Cn 16' R
Mer	Direct	Jul 5 1948	05:59	28° Ge 18' D
Ven	Direct	Jul 15 1948	22:22	24° Ge 38' D
Jup	Direct	Aug 15 1948	17:11	19° Sg 06' D
Mer	Retrograde	Oct 7 1948	18:15	05° Sc 24' R
Mer	Direct	Oct 28 1948	15:58	19° Li 46' D
Sat	Retrograde	Dec 16 1948	15:22	06° Vi 12' R
Mer	Retrograde	Jan 24 1949	13:10	20° Aq 12' R
Mer	Direct	Feb 14 1949	16:38	04° Aq 34' D
Sat	Direct	May 1 1949	00:41	29° Le 19' D
Jup	Retrograde	May 20 1949	08:02	02° Aq 10' R
Mer	Retrograde	May 22 1949	19:11	17° Ge 13' R
Mer	Direct	Jun 15 1949	17:03	08° Ge 40' D
Jup	Direct	Sep 18 1949	11:13	22° Cp 20' D

Mer	Retrograde	Sep 20 1949	20:43	19° Li 06' R
Mer	Direct	Oct 12 1949	12:38	03° Li 57' D
Sat	Retrograde	Dec 29 1949	19:44	19° Vi 26' R
Mer	Retrograde	Jan 8 1950	09:47	04° Aq 07' R
Ven	Retrograde	Jan 10 1950	06:33	18° Aq 44' R
Mer	Direct	Jan 28 1950	21:56	18° Cp 04' D
Mar	Retrograde	Feb 11 1950	22:36	11° Li 02' R
Ven	Direct	Feb 20 1950	10:59	03° Aq 06' D
Mar	Direct	May 3 1950	08:48	22° Vi 00' D
Mer	Retrograde	May 3 1950	08:59	27° Ta 31' R
Sat	Direct	May 15 1950	01:02	12° Vi 35' D
Mer	Direct	May 27 1950	05:22	18° Ta 31' D
Jup	Retrograde	Jun 26 1950	16:21	07° Pi 27' R
Mer	Retrograde	Sep 3 1950	17:07	02° Li 25' R
Mer	Direct	Sep 26 1950	04:51	17° Vi 58' D
Jup	Direct	Oct 23 1950	22:42	27° Aq 35' D
Mer	Retrograde	Dec 23 1950	07:40	18° Cp 10' R
Sat	Retrograde	Jan 11 1951	17:14	02° Li 22' R
Mer	Direct	Jan 12 1951	08:27	01° Cp 56' D
Mer	Retrograde	Apr 14 1951	10:44	08° Ta 33' R
Mer	Direct	May 8 1951	04:45	28° Ar 21' D
Sat	Direct	May 28 1951	19:03	25° Vi 32' D
Jup	Retrograde	Aug 3 1951	23:21	14° Ar 11' R
Ven	Retrograde	Aug 13 1951	00:45	18° Vi 20' R
Mer	Retrograde	Aug 17 1951	06:58	15° Vi 09' R
Mer	Direct	Sep 9 1951	13:15	01° Vi 39' D
Ven	Direct	Sep 24 1951	17:56	02° Vi 06' D
Jup	Direct	Nov 29 1951	20:56	04° Ar 15' D
Mer	Retrograde	Dec 7 1951	04:49	02° Cp 19' R
Mer	Direct	Dec 26 1951	23:31	16° Sg 02' D
Sat	Retrograde	Jan 24 1952	08:51	14° Li 59' R
Mar	Retrograde	Mar 25 1952	04:04	18° Sc 28' R
Mer	Retrograde	Mar 26 1952	06:48	20° Ar 24' R
Mer	Direct	Apr 18 1952	18:26	08° Ar 41' D
Mar	Direct	Jun 9 1952	19:42	01° Sc 10' D
Sat	Direct	Jun 10 1952	05:41	08° Li 12' D
Mer	Retrograde	Jul 29 1952	13:25	27° Le 10' R
Mer	Direct	Aug 22 1952	09:48	14° Le 54' D
Jup	Retrograde	Sep 9 1952	11:57	20° Ta 59' R
Mer	Retrograde	Nov 19 1952	23:36	16° Sg 30' R
Mer	Direct	Dec 9 1952	18:21	00° Sg 17' D

Jup	Direct	Jan 5 1953	00:09	10° Ta 59' D
Sat	Retrograde	Feb 4 1953	18:29	27° Li 18' R
Mer	Retrograde	Mar 8 1953	20:38	02° Ar 59' R
Ven	Retrograde	Mar 22 1953	20:48	01° Ta 21' R
Mer	Direct	Mar 31 1953	20:29	19° Pi 48' D
Ven	Direct	May 4 1953	05:30	14° Ar 58' D
Sat	Direct	Jun 23 1953	09:25	20° Li 33' D
Mer	Retrograde	Jul 11 1953	10:18	08° Le 22' R
Mer	Direct	Aug 4 1953	14:15	27° Cn 30' D
Jup	Retrograde	Oct 14 1953	19:08	26° Ge 29' R
Mer	Retrograde	Nov 3 1953	14:43	00° Sg 41' R
Mer	Direct	Nov 23 1953	15:48	14° Sc 36' D
Jup	Direct	Feb 10 1954	01:54	16° Ge 25' D
Sat	Retrograde	Feb 16 1954	22:12	09° Sc 21' R
Mer	Retrograde	Feb 20 1954	00:27	16° Pi 06' R
Mer	Direct	Mar 14 1954	08:00	01° Pi 43' D
Mar	Retrograde	May 23 1954	05:43	08° Cp 32' R
Mer	Retrograde	Jun 22 1954	19:04	18° Cn 50' R
Sat	Direct	Jul 6 1954	07:17	02° Sc 39' D
Mer	Direct	Jul 16 1954	23:45	09° Cn 18' D
Mar	Direct	Jul 29 1954	08:16	25° Sg 35' D
Mer	Retrograde	Oct 18 1954	01:18	14° Sc 45' R
Ven	Retrograde	Oct 25 1954	09:35	00° Sg 04' R
Mer	Direct	Nov 7 1954	14:22	28° Li 55' D
Jup	Retrograde	Nov 16 1954	19:26	29° Cn 57' R
Ven	Direct	Dec 5 1954	15:35	14° Sc 40' D
Mer	Retrograde	Feb 3 1955	13:47	29° Aq 39' R
Mer	Direct	Feb 25 1955	03:10	14° Aq 22' D
Sat	Retrograde	Feb 28 1955	21:42	21° Sc 11' R
Jup	Direct	Mar 16 1955	13:03	19° Cn 53' D
Mer	Retrograde	Jun 3 1955	15:40	28° Ge 50' R
Mer	Direct	Jun 27 1955	16:04	20° Ge 10' D
Sat	Direct	Jul 18 1955	23:36	14° Sc 30' D
Mer	Retrograde	Oct 1 1955	06:52	28° Li 38' R
Mer	Direct	Oct 22 1955	12:15	13° Li 10' D
Jup	Retrograde	Dec 17 1955	20:45	01° Vi 30' R
Mer	Retrograde	Jan 18 1956	08:45	13° Aq 26' R
Mer	Direct	Feb 8 1956	05:03	27° Cp 36' D
Sat	Retrograde	Mar 11 1956	19:44	02° Sg 49' R
Jup	Direct	Apr 17 1956	05:25	21° Le 29' D
Mer	Retrograde	May 14 1956	05:06	08° Ge 52' R

Ven	Retrograde	May 31 1956	11:01	09° Cn 01' R
Mer	Direct	Jun 7 1956	01:29	00° Ge 14' D
Ven	Direct	Jul 13 1956	14:15	22° Ge 30' D
Sat	Direct	Jul 30 1956	10:14	26° Sc 10' D
Mar	Retrograde	Aug 10 1956	09:19	23° Pi 39' R
Mer	Retrograde	Sep 13 1956	07:01	12° Li 11' R
Mer	Direct	Oct 5 1956	07:13	27° Vi 17' D
Mar	Direct	Oct 10 1956	03:03	13° Pi 09' D
Mer	Retrograde	Jan 1 1957	06:15	27° Cp 25' R
Jup	Retrograde	Jan 16 1957	01:27	01° Li 48' R
Mer	Direct	Jan 21 1957	12:49	11° Cp 16' D
Sat	Retrograde	Mar 23 1957	16:24	14° Sg 18' R
Mer	Retrograde	Apr 24 1957	22:26	19° Ta 26' R
Mer	Direct	May 18 1957	17:59	10° Ta 00' D
Jup	Direct	May 18 1957	18:42	21° Vi 50' D
Sat	Direct	Aug 11 1957	15:14	07° Sg 41' D
Mer	Retrograde	Aug 27 1957	00:58	25° Vi 14' R
Mer	Direct	Sep 18 1957	20:30	11° Vi 10' D
Mer	Retrograde	Dec 16 1957	03:58	11° Cp 31' R
Mer	Direct	Jan 5 1958	01:32	25° Sg 15' D
Ven	Retrograde	Jan 7 1958	19:44	16° Aq 18' R
Jup	Retrograde	Feb 15 1958	07:15	01° Sc 40' R
Ven	Direct	Feb 17 1958	23:12	00° Aq 42' D
Sat	Retrograde	Apr 4 1958	11:41	25° Sg 42' R
Mer	Retrograde	Apr 6 1958	07:18	00° Ta 50' R
Mer	Direct	Apr 29 1958	23:50	20° Ar 00' D
Jup	Direct	Jun 18 1958	18:15	21° Li 45' D
Mer	Retrograde	Aug 9 1958	11:41	07° Vi 41' R
Sat	Direct	Aug 23 1958	16:23	19° Sg 06' D
Mer	Direct	Sep 2 1958	00:35	24° Le 42' D
Mar	Retrograde	Oct 10 1958	02:44	02° Ge 32' R
Mer	Retrograde	Nov 30 1958	00:09	25° Sg 41' R
Mer	Direct	Dec 19 1958	18:19	09° Sg 26' D
Mar	Direct	Dec 19 1958	23:38	16° Ta 35' D
Jup	Retrograde	Mar 18 1959	14:28	01° Sg 59' R
Mer	Retrograde	Mar 19 1959	11:27	13° Ar 01' R
Mer	Direct	Apr 11 1959	18:47	00° Ar 39' D
Sat	Retrograde	Apr 16 1959	07:14	07° Cp 04' R
Jup	Direct	Jul 20 1959	00:29	22° Sc 08' D
Mer	Retrograde	Jul 22 1959	13:57	19° Le 22' R
Ven	Retrograde	Aug 10 1959	16:13	16° Vi 07' R

Mer	Direct	Aug 15 1959	14:59	07° Le 41' D
Sat	Direct	Sep 4 1959	16:08	00° Cp 28' D
Ven	Direct	Sep 22 1959	10:11	29° Le 52' D
Mer	Retrograde	Nov 13 1959	17:30	09° Sg 53' R
Mer	Direct	Dec 3 1959	14:18	23° Sc 42' D
Mer	Retrograde	Mar 1 1960	08:03	25° Pi 51' R
Mer	Direct	Mar 24 1960	00:58	12° Pi 07' D
Jup	Retrograde	Apr 19 1960	21:23	03° Cp 37' R
Sat	Retrograde	Apr 27 1960	05:48	18° Cp 26' R
Mer	Retrograde	Jul 3 1960	06:10	00° Le 14' R
Mer	Direct	Jul 27 1960	11:18	19° Cn 58' D
Jup	Direct	Aug 20 1960	08:58	23° Sg 47' D
Sat	Direct	Sep 15 1960	14:22	11° Cp 49' D
Mer	Retrograde	Oct 27 1960	06:55	24° Sc 01' R
Mer	Direct	Nov 16 1960	12:19	08° Sc 01' D
Mar	Retrograde	Nov 20 1960	09:55	18° Cn 39' R
Mar	Direct	Feb 5 1961	19:40	00° Cn 00' D
Mer	Retrograde	Feb 12 1961	16:25	09° Pi 10' R
Mer	Direct	Mar 6 1961	16:09	24° Aq 21' D
Ven	Retrograde	Mar 20 1961	13:09	29° Ar 05' R
Ven	Direct	May 1 1961	21:12	12° Ar 45' D
Sat	Retrograde	May 9 1961	08:21	29° Cp 51' R
Jup	Retrograde	May 25 1961	11:06	07° Aq 09' R
Mer	Retrograde	Jun 14 1961	10:00	10° Cn 27' R
Mer	Direct	Jul 8 1961	12:30	01° Cn 21' D
Jup	Direct	Sep 23 1961	07:33	27° Cp 19' D
Sat	Direct	Sep 27 1961	10:59	23° Cp 14' D
Mer	Retrograde	Oct 10 1961	15:35	08° Sc 01' R
Mer	Direct	Oct 31 1961	10:53	22° Li 19' D
Mer	Retrograde	Jan 27 1962	08:24	22° Aq 48' R
Mer	Direct	Feb 17 1962	14:28	07° Aq 15' D
Sat	Retrograde	May 21 1962	14:36	11° Aq 24' R
Mer	Retrograde	May 26 1962	02:04	20° Ge 23' R
Mer	Direct	Jun 19 1962	00:41	11° Ge 51' D
Jup	Retrograde	Jul 2 1962	01:07	12° Pi 41' R
Mer	Retrograde	Sep 23 1962	18:46	21° Li 46' R
Sat	Direct	Oct 9 1962	07:55	04° Aq 46' D
Mer	Direct	Oct 15 1962	07:57	06° Li 31' D
Ven	Retrograde	Oct 22 1962	21:12	27° Sc 37' R
Jup	Direct	Oct 29 1962	02:49	02° Pi 49' D
Ven	Direct	Dec 3 1962	04:24	12° Sc 13' D

Mar	Retrograde	Dec 25 1962	23:00	24° Le 48' R
Mer	Retrograde	Jan 11 1963	04:40	06° Aq 41' R
Mer	Direct	Jan 31 1963	18:51	20° Cp 42' D
Mar	Direct	Mar 16 1963	10:13	05° Le 20' D
Mer	Retrograde	May 6 1963	15:24	00° Ge 37' R
Mer	Direct	May 30 1963	11:45	21° Ta 44' D
Sat	Retrograde	Jun 3 1963	01:29	23° Aq 07' R
Jup	Retrograde	Aug 9 1963	08:02	19° Ar 29' R
Mer	Retrograde	Sep 6 1963	16:03	05° Li 08' R
Mer	Direct	Sep 29 1963	00:57	20° Vi 34' D
Sat	Direct	Oct 21 1963	08:07	16° Aq 27' D
Jup	Direct	Dec 5 1963	02:42	09° Ar 32' D
Mer	Retrograde	Dec 26 1963	02:33	20° Cp 43' R
Mer	Direct	Jan 15 1964	04:35	04° Cp 31' D
Mer	Retrograde	Apr 16 1964	14:44	11° Ta 31' R
Mer	Direct	May 10 1964	09:03	01° Ta 31' D
Ven	Retrograde	May 29 1964	03:25	06° Cn 52' R
Sat	Retrograde	Jun 14 1964	19:06	05° Pi 02' R
Ven	Direct	Jul 11 1964	05:58	20° Ge 22' D
Mer	Retrograde	Aug 19 1964	07:08	17° Vi 57' R
Mer	Direct	Sep 11 1964	10:41	04° Vi 18' D
Jup	Retrograde	Sep 14 1964	11:19	26° Ta 08' R
Sat	Direct	Nov 1 1964	11:59	28° Aq 21' D
Mer	Retrograde	Dec 8 1964	23:58	04° Cp 52' R
Mer	Direct	Dec 28 1964	19:07	18° Sg 35' D
Jup	Direct	Jan 10 1965	01:47	16° Ta 06' D
Mar	Retrograde	Jan 28 1965	15:27	28° Vi 03' R
Mer	Retrograde	Mar 29 1965	07:46	23° Ar 15' R
Mar	Direct	Apr 19 1965	14:50	08° Vi 43' D
Mer	Direct	Apr 21 1965	20:55	11° Ar 46' D
Sat	Retrograde	Jun 27 1965	20:28	17° Pi 13' R
Mer	Retrograde	Aug 1 1965	14:50	00° Vi 05' R
Mer	Direct	Aug 25 1965	09:18	17° Le 37' D
Jup	Retrograde	Oct 19 1965	11:56	01° Cn 19' R
Sat	Direct	Nov 13 1965	19:27	10° Pi 29' D
Mer	Retrograde	Nov 22 1965	19:08	19° Sg 03' R
Mer	Direct	Dec 12 1965	13:33	02° Sg 49' D
Ven	Retrograde	Jan 5 1966	09:16	13° Aq 50' R
Jup	Direct	Feb 14 1966	23:28	21° Ge 15' D
Ven	Direct	Feb 15 1966	11:38	28° Cp 14' D
Mer	Retrograde	Mar 11 1966	19:12	05° Ar 44' R

Mer	Direct	Apr 3 1966	21:18	22° Pi 45' D
Sat	Retrograde	Jul 11 1966	04:56	29° Pi 41' R
Mer	Retrograde	Jul 14 1966	13:08	11° Le 25' R
Mer	Direct	Aug 7 1966	16:35	00° Le 21' D
Mer	Retrograde	Nov 6 1966	10:48	03° Sg 15' R
Jup	Retrograde	Nov 21 1966	02:50	04° Le 29' R
Sat	Direct	Nov 26 1966	07:22	22° Pi 55' D
Mer	Direct	Nov 26 1966	10:42	17° Sc 08' D
Mer	Retrograde	Feb 22 1967	21:19	18° Pi 47' R
Mar	Retrograde	Mar 8 1967	10:39	03° Sc 12' R
Mer	Direct	Mar 17 1967	07:21	04° Pi 33' D
Jup	Direct	Mar 21 1967	01:44	24° Cn 26' D
Mar	Direct	May 26 1967	02:27	14° Li 59' D
Mer	Retrograde	Jun 25 1967	23:46	21° Cn 58' R
Mer	Direct	Jul 20 1967	04:56	12° Cn 16' D
Sat	Retrograde	Jul 24 1967	20:07	12° Ar 28' R
Ven	Retrograde	Aug 8 1967	07:27	13° Vi 54' R
Ven	Direct	Sep 20 1967	02:30	27° Le 38' D
Mer	Retrograde	Oct 20 1967	22:08	17° Sc 20' R
Mer	Direct	Nov 10 1967	09:08	01° Sc 27' D
Sat	Direct	Dec 9 1967	01:59	05° Ar 39' D
Jup	Retrograde	Dec 22 1967	02:22	05° Vi 50' R
Mer	Retrograde	Feb 6 1968	09:33	02° Pi 17' R
Mer	Direct	Feb 28 1968	01:29	17° Aq 07' D
Jup	Direct	Apr 21 1968	15:39	25° Le 50' D
Mer	Retrograde	Jun 5 1968	22:11	02° Cn 01' R
Mer	Direct	Jun 29 1968	23:03	23° Ge 16' D
Sat	Retrograde	Aug 6 1968	17:41	25° Ar 33' R
Mer	Retrograde	Oct 3 1968	04:33	01° Sc 14' R
Mer	Direct	Oct 24 1968	07:10	15° Li 43' D
Sat	Direct	Dec 21 1968	04:04	18° Ar 42' D
Mer	Retrograde	Jan 20 1969	03:49	16° Aq 01' R
Jup	Retrograde	Jan 20 1969	04:50	06° Li 03' R
Mer	Direct	Feb 10 1969	02:32	00° Aq 16' D
Ven	Retrograde	Mar 18 1969	04:47	26° Ar 50' R
Mar	Retrograde	Apr 27 1969	04:23	16° Sg 46' R
Ven	Direct	Apr 29 1969	12:15	10° Ar 30' D
Mer	Retrograde	May 17 1969	12:00	12° Ge 01' R
Jup	Direct	May 23 1969	00:40	26° Vi 06' D
Mer	Direct	Jun 10 1969	08:42	03° Ge 26' D
Mar	Direct	Jul 7 1969	23:04	01° Sg 42' D

Sat	Retrograde	Aug 20 1969	21:10	08° Ta 57' R
Mer	Retrograde	Sep 16 1969	05:35	14° Li 51' R
Mer	Direct	Oct 8 1969	02:46	29° Vi 52' D
Sat	Direct	Jan 3 1970	13:11	02° Ta 03' D
Mer	Retrograde	Jan 4 1970	01:03	29° Cp 59' R
Mer	Direct	Jan 24 1970	09:31	13° Cp 52' D
Jup	Retrograde	Feb 19 1970	14:21	05° Sc 58' R
Mer	Retrograde	Apr 28 1970	03:45	22° Ta 29' R
Mer	Direct	May 21 1970	23:42	13° Ta 13' D
Jup	Direct	Jun 23 1970	02:05	26° Li 04' D
Mer	Retrograde	Aug 30 1970	00:22	28° Vi 00' R
Sat	Retrograde	Sep 4 1970	06:08	22° Ta 37' R
Mer	Direct	Sep 21 1970	17:11	13° Vi 47' D
Ven	Retrograde	Oct 20 1970	08:53	25° Sc 13' R
Ven	Direct	Nov 30 1970	17:01	09° Sc 47' D
Mer	Retrograde	Dec 18 1970	22:52	14° Cp 04' R
Mer	Direct	Jan 7 1971	21:29	27° Sg 50' D
Sat	Direct	Jan 17 1971	04:32	15° Ta 42' D
Jup	Retrograde	Mar 23 1971	03:55	06° Sg 27' R
Mer	Retrograde	Apr 9 1971	10:05	03° Ta 46' R
Mer	Direct	May 3 1971	03:19	23° Ar 09' D
Mar	Retrograde	Jul 10 1971	23:30	21° Aq 57' R
Jup	Direct	Jul 24 1971	11:23	26° Sc 36' D
Mer	Retrograde	Aug 12 1971	12:07	10° Vi 33' R
Mer	Direct	Sep 4 1971	22:55	27° Le 23' D
Mar	Direct	Sep 9 1971	06:45	11° Aq 54' D
Sat	Retrograde	Sep 18 1971	18:37	06° Ge 32' R
Mer	Retrograde	Dec 2 1971	19:25	28° Sg 14' R
Mer	Direct	Dec 22 1971	13:40	11° Sg 58' D
Sat	Direct	Jan 31 1972	02:05	29° Ta 35' D
Mer	Retrograde	Mar 21 1972	11:32	15° Ar 51' R
Mer	Direct	Apr 13 1972	20:23	03° Ar 41' D
Jup	Retrograde	Apr 24 1972	16:55	08° Cp 19' R
Ven	Retrograde	May 26 1972	20:10	04° Cn 44' R
Ven	Direct	Jul 8 1972	21:54	18° Ge 13' D
Mer	Retrograde	Jul 24 1972	15:57	22° Le 21' R
Mer	Direct	Aug 17 1972	15:32	10° Le 28' D
Jup	Direct	Aug 25 1972	00:07	28° Sg 29' D
Sat	Retrograde	Oct 2 1972	08:26	20° Ge 36' R
Mer	Retrograde	Nov 15 1972	13:20	12° Sg 27' R
Mer	Direct	Dec 5 1972	09:16	26° Sc 15' D

Sat	Direct	Feb 13 1973	05:05	13° Ge 38' D
Mer	Retrograde	Mar 4 1973	05:52	28° Pi 35' R
Mer	Direct	Mar 27 1973	01:13	15° Pi 01' D
Jup	Retrograde	May 30 1973	14:19	12° Aq 08' R
Mer	Retrograde	Jul 6 1973	09:55	03° Le 20' R
Mer	Direct	Jul 30 1973	14:41	22° Cn 52' D
Mar	Retrograde	Sep 19 1973	16:15	09° Ta 16' R
Jup	Direct	Sep 28 1973	05:38	02° Aq 17' D
Sat	Retrograde	Oct 16 1973	21:16	04° Cn 45' R
Mer	Retrograde	Oct 30 1973	03:22	26° Sc 35' R
Mer	Direct	Nov 19 1973	07:06	10° Sc 34' D
Mar	Direct	Nov 25 1973	17:04	25° Ar 18' D
Ven	Retrograde	Jan 2 1974	23:03	11° Aq 22' R
Ven	Direct	Feb 13 1974	00:25	25° Cp 49' D
Mer	Retrograde	Feb 15 1974	12:38	11° Pi 50' R
Sat	Direct	Feb 27 1974	12:58	27° Ge 47' D
Mer	Direct	Mar 9 1974	15:09	27° Aq 09' D
Mer	Retrograde	Jun 17 1974	15:32	13° Cn 38' R
Jup	Retrograde	Jul 7 1974	08:37	17° Pi 52' R
Mer	Direct	Jul 11 1974	18:50	04° Cn 24' D
Mer	Retrograde	Oct 13 1974	12:42	10° Sc 38' R
Sat	Retrograde	Oct 31 1974	06:44	18° Cn 54' R
Jup	Direct	Nov 3 1974	04:48	07° Pi 59' D
Mer	Direct	Nov 3 1974	05:44	24° Li 53' D
Mer	Retrograde	Jan 30 1975	03:41	25° Aq 25' R
Mer	Direct	Feb 20 1975	12:21	09° Aq 58' D
Sat	Direct	Mar 13 1975	23:50	11° Cn 57' D
Mer	Retrograde	May 29 1975	08:55	23° Ge 35' R
Mer	Direct	Jun 22 1975	08:13	15° Ge 01' D
Ven	Retrograde	Aug 5 1975	22:17	11° Vi 42' R
Jup	Retrograde	Aug 14 1975	11:48	24° Ar 42' R
Ven	Direct	Sep 17 1975	18:43	25° Le 26' D
Mer	Retrograde	Sep 26 1975	16:39	24° Li 25' R
Mer	Direct	Oct 18 1975	03:08	09° Li 06' D
Mar	Retrograde	Nov 6 1975	04:54	02° Cn 40' R
Sat	Retrograde	Nov 14 1975	11:31	02° Le 59' R
Jup	Direct	Dec 10 1975	04:57	14° Ar 45' D
Mer	Retrograde	Jan 13 1976	23:35	09° Aq 17' R
Mar	Direct	Jan 20 1976	14:18	14° Ge 44' D
Mer	Direct	Feb 3 1976	15:50	23° Cp 21' D
Sat	Direct	Mar 27 1976	11:19	26° Cn 02' D

Mer	Retrograde	May 8 1976	21:58	03° Ge 44' R
Mer	Direct	Jun 1 1976	18:14	24° Ta 57' D
Mer	Retrograde	Sep 8 1976	14:58	07° Li 51' R
Jup	Retrograde	Sep 19 1976	11:05	01° Ge 12' R
Mer	Direct	Sep 30 1976	20:53	23° Vi 10' D
Sat	Retrograde	Nov 27 1976	10:39	16° Le 53' R
Mer	Retrograde	Dec 27 1976	21:27	23° Cp 18' R
Jup	Direct	Jan 15 1977	03:29	21° Ta 10' D
Mer	Direct	Jan 17 1977	00:54	07° Cp 07' D
Ven	Retrograde	Mar 15 1977	19:58	24° Ar 33' R
Sat	Direct	Apr 10 1977	21:31	09° Le 57' D
Mer	Retrograde	Apr 19 1977	19:04	14° Ta 30' R
Ven	Direct	Apr 27 1977	02:45	08° Ar 15' D
Mer	Direct	May 13 1977	13:45	04° Ta 43' D
Mer	Retrograde	Aug 22 1977	07:12	20° Vi 46' R
Mer	Direct	Sep 14 1977	07:57	06° Vi 58' D
Jup	Retrograde	Oct 24 1977	02:50	06° Cn 08' R
Sat	Retrograde	Dec 11 1977	03:23	00° Vi 33' R
Mer	Retrograde	Dec 11 1977	19:04	07° Cp 26' R
Mar	Retrograde	Dec 12 1977	12:02	11° Le 34' R
Mer	Direct	Dec 31 1977	14:55	21° Sg 09' D
Jup	Direct	Feb 19 1978	17:44	26° Ge 04' D
Mar	Direct	Mar 2 1978	02:51	22° Cn 17' D
Mer	Retrograde	Apr 1 1978	09:11	26° Ar 07' R
Mer	Direct	Apr 24 1978	23:42	14° Ar 52' D
Sat	Direct	Apr 25 1978	04:13	23° Le 39' D
Mer	Retrograde	Aug 4 1978	16:02	03° Vi 00' R
Mer	Direct	Aug 28 1978	08:35	20° Le 21' D
Ven	Retrograde	Oct 17 1978	20:56	22° Sc 48' R
Jup	Retrograde	Nov 25 1978	12:59	09° Le 04' R
Mer	Retrograde	Nov 25 1978	14:35	21° Sg 37' R
Ven	Direct	Nov 28 1978	06:07	07° Sc 20' D
Mer	Direct	Dec 15 1978	08:50	05° Sg 22' D
Sat	Retrograde	Dec 24 1978	13:02	13° Vi 56' R
Mer	Retrograde	Mar 14 1979	18:09	08° Ar 30' R
Jup	Direct	Mar 25 1979	17:00	29° Cn 00' D
Mer	Direct	Apr 6 1979	22:15	25° Pi 44' D
Sat	Direct	May 9 1979	06:19	07° Vi 05' D
Mer	Retrograde	Jul 17 1979	15:36	14° Le 27' R
Mer	Direct	Aug 10 1979	18:26	03° Le 10' D
Mer	Retrograde	Nov 9 1979	06:48	05° Sg 48' R

Mer	Direct	Nov 29 1979	05:34	19° Sc 41' D
Jup	Retrograde	Dec 26 1979	07:24	10° Vi 15' R
Sat	Retrograde	Jan 6 1980	14:33	27° Vi 01' R
Mar	Retrograde	Jan 15 1980	23:07	15° Vi 21' R
Mer	Retrograde	Feb 25 1980	18:26	21° Pi 29' R
Mer	Direct	Mar 19 1980	06:53	07° Pi 25' D
Mar	Direct	Apr 6 1980	01:21	25° Le 52' D
Jup	Direct	Apr 26 1980	00:52	00° Vi 14' D
Sat	Direct	May 22 1980	03:23	20° Vi 12' D
Ven	Retrograde	May 24 1980	13:08	02° Cn 35' R
Mer	Retrograde	Jun 28 1980	04:07	25° Cn 07' R
Ven	Direct	Jul 6 1980	14:11	16° Ge 04' D
Mer	Direct	Jul 22 1980	09:31	15° Cn 13' D
Mer	Retrograde	Oct 22 1980	18:52	19° Sc 55' R
Mer	Direct	Nov 12 1980	03:49	04° Sc 00' D
Sat	Retrograde	Jan 18 1981	08:14	09° Li 47' R
Jup	Retrograde	Jan 24 1981	11:51	10° Li 23' R
Mer	Retrograde	Feb 8 1981	05:24	04° Pi 54' R
Mer	Direct	Mar 2 1981	00:00	19° Aq 52' D
Jup	Direct	May 27 1981	10:38	00° Li 27' D
Sat	Direct	Jun 4 1981	18:27	03° Li 00' D
Mer	Retrograde	Jun 9 1981	04:30	05° Cn 12' R
Mer	Direct	Jul 3 1981	05:52	26° Ge 21' D
Mer	Retrograde	Oct 6 1981	02:08	03° Sc 51' R
Mer	Direct	Oct 27 1981	02:03	18° Li 17' D
Ven	Retrograde	Dec 31 1981	12:43	08° Aq 54' R
Mer	Retrograde	Jan 22 1982	22:56	18° Aq 37' R
Sat	Retrograde	Jan 30 1982	19:47	22° Li 15' R
Ven	Direct	Feb 10 1982	13:33	23° Cp 22' D
Mer	Direct	Feb 13 1982	00:11	02° Aq 56' D
Mar	Retrograde	Feb 20 1982	12:07	19° Li 11' R
Jup	Retrograde	Feb 23 1982	22:13	10° Sc 20' R
Mar	Direct	May 11 1982	11:32	00° Li 23' D
Mer	Retrograde	May 20 1982	19:01	15° Ge 10' R
Mer	Direct	Jun 13 1982	16:15	06° Ge 37' D
Sat	Direct	Jun 18 1982	02:53	15° Li 30' D
Jup	Direct	Jun 27 1982	10:27	00° Sc 26' D
Mer	Retrograde	Sep 19 1982	03:57	17° Li 31' R
Mer	Direct	Oct 10 1982	22:15	02° Li 26' D
Mer	Retrograde	Jan 6 1983	19:53	02° Aq 33' R
Mer	Direct	Jan 27 1983	06:19	16° Cp 29' D

Sat	Retrograde	Feb 12 1983	03:05	04° Sc 26' R
Jup	Retrograde	Mar 27 1983	16:35	10° Sg 55' R
Mer	Retrograde	May 1 1983	09:30	25° Ta 33' R
Mer	Direct	May 25 1983	05:43	16° Ta 26' D
Sat	Direct	Jul 1 1983	04:01	27° Li 43' D
Jup	Direct	Jul 28 1983	23:12	01° Sg 04' D
Ven	Retrograde	Aug 3 1983	12:41	09° Vi 30' R
Mer	Retrograde	Sep 1 1983	23:35	00° Li 44' R
Ven	Direct	Sep 15 1983	10:20	23° Le 12' D
Mer	Direct	Sep 24 1983	13:43	16° Vi 23' D
Mer	Retrograde	Dec 21 1983	17:46	16° Cp 38' R
Mer	Direct	Jan 10 1984	17:30	00° Cp 24' D
Sat	Retrograde	Feb 24 1984	06:04	16° Sc 23' R
Mar	Retrograde	Apr 5 1984	05:15	28° Sc 21' R
Mer	Retrograde	Apr 11 1984	13:17	06° Ta 42' R
Jup	Retrograde	Apr 29 1984	11:10	12° Cp 58' R
Mer	Direct	May 5 1984	07:01	26° Ar 19' D
Mar	Direct	Jun 19 1984	11:10	11° Sc 42' D
Sat	Direct	Jul 12 1984	22:26	09° Sc 42' D
Mer	Retrograde	Aug 14 1984	12:28	13° Vi 24' R
Jup	Direct	Aug 29 1984	15:09	03° Cp 08' D
Mer	Direct	Sep 6 1984	20:55	00° Vi 03' D
Mer	Retrograde	Dec 4 1984	14:40	00° Cp 48' R
Mer	Direct	Dec 24 1984	09:04	14° Sg 31' D
Sat	Retrograde	Mar 7 1985	04:51	28° Sc 08' R
Ven	Retrograde	Mar 13 1985	11:12	22° Ar 18' R
Mer	Retrograde	Mar 24 1985	11:54	18° Ar 39' R
Mer	Direct	Apr 16 1985	22:16	06° Ar 44' D
Ven	Direct	Apr 24 1985	17:06	06° Ar 00' D
Jup	Retrograde	Jun 4 1985	14:21	16° Aq 58' R
Sat	Direct	Jul 25 1985	11:19	21° Sc 28' D
Mer	Retrograde	Jul 27 1985	17:46	25° Le 19' R
Mer	Direct	Aug 20 1985	15:41	13° Le 13' D
Jup	Direct	Oct 3 1985	00:37	07° Aq 07' D
Mer	Retrograde	Nov 18 1985	09:03	15° Sg 00' R
Mer	Direct	Dec 8 1985	04:16	28° Sc 47' D
Mer	Retrograde	Mar 7 1986	03:50	01° Ar 18' R
Sat	Retrograde	Mar 19 1986	00:53	09° Sg 42' R
Mer	Direct	Mar 30 1986	01:37	17° Pi 56' D
Mar	Retrograde	Jun 8 1986	16:16	23° Cp 07' R
Mer	Retrograde	Jul 9 1986	13:21	06° Le 25' R

Jup	Retrograde	Jul 12 1986	09:32	22° Pi 51' R
Mer	Direct	Aug 2 1986	17:42	25° Cn 44' D
Sat	Direct	Aug 6 1986	20:19	03° Sg 04' D
Mar	Direct	Aug 12 1986	00:39	11° Cp 25' D
Ven	Retrograde	Oct 15 1986	09:32	20° Sc 23' R
Mer	Retrograde	Nov 1 1986	23:41	29° Sc 09' R
Jup	Direct	Nov 8 1986	01:58	12° Pi 58' D
Mer	Direct	Nov 22 1986	01:56	13° Sc 06' D
Ven	Direct	Nov 25 1986	19:43	04° Sc 54' D
Mer	Retrograde	Feb 18 1987	09:01	14° Pi 29' R
Mer	Direct	Mar 12 1987	14:16	29° Aq 57' D
Sat	Retrograde	Mar 30 1987	20:43	21° Sg 10' R
Mer	Retrograde	Jun 20 1987	20:39	16° Cn 48' R
Mer	Direct	Jul 15 1987	00:46	07° Cn 25' D
Sat	Direct	Aug 19 1987	00:54	14° Sg 32' D
Jup	Retrograde	Aug 19 1987	13:20	29° Ar 44' R
Mer	Retrograde	Oct 16 1987	09:39	13° Sc 12' R
Mer	Direct	Nov 6 1987	00:32	27° Li 25' D
Jup	Direct	Dec 15 1987	04:41	19° Ar 46' D
Mer	Retrograde	Feb 1 1988	23:11	28° Aq 03' R
Mer	Direct	Feb 23 1988	10:24	12° Aq 41' D
Sat	Retrograde	Apr 10 1988	17:41	02° Cp 33' R
Ven	Retrograde	May 22 1988	06:23	00° Cn 27' R
Mer	Retrograde	May 31 1988	15:37	26° Ge 47' R
Mer	Direct	Jun 24 1988	15:34	18° Ge 09' D
Ven	Direct	Jul 4 1988	07:05	13° Ge 56' D
Mar	Retrograde	Aug 26 1988	07:36	11° Ar 28' R
Sat	Direct	Aug 30 1988	01:19	25° Sg 56' D
Jup	Retrograde	Sep 24 1988	06:37	06° Ge 08' R
Mer	Retrograde	Sep 28 1988	14:30	27° Li 03' R
Mer	Direct	Oct 19 1988	22:15	11° Li 40' D
Mar	Direct	Oct 27 1988	22:05	29° Pi 53' D
Mer	Retrograde	Jan 15 1989	18:39	11° Aq 53' R
Jup	Direct	Jan 19 1989	22:51	26° Ta 05' D
Mer	Direct	Feb 5 1989	13:01	25° Cp 59' D
Sat	Retrograde	Apr 22 1989	15:12	13° Cp 56' R
Mer	Retrograde	May 12 1989	04:47	06° Ge 51' R
Mer	Direct	Jun 5 1989	01:02	28° Ta 10' D
Sat	Direct	Sep 10 1989	23:05	07° Cp 18' D
Mer	Retrograde	Sep 11 1989	13:51	10° Li 33' R
Mer	Direct	Oct 3 1989	16:41	25° Vi 45' D

Jup	Retrograde	Oct 28 1989	16:33	10° Cn 53' R
Ven	Retrograde	Dec 29 1989	01:47	06° Aq 25' R
Mer	Retrograde	Dec 30 1989	16:22	25° Cp 53' R
Mer	Direct	Jan 19 1990	21:25	09° Cp 43' D
Ven	Direct	Feb 8 1990	02:13	20° Cp 56' D
Jup	Direct	Feb 24 1990	11:27	00° Cn 48' D
Mer	Retrograde	Apr 22 1990	23:50	17° Ta 31' R
Sat	Retrograde	May 4 1990	14:47	25° Cp 20' R
Mer	Direct	May 16 1990	18:57	07° Ta 55' D
Mer	Retrograde	Aug 25 1990	07:02	23° Vi 33' R
Mer	Direct	Sep 17 1990	04:59	09° Vi 36' D
Sat	Direct	Sep 22 1990	20:43	18° Cp 42' D
Mar	Retrograde	Oct 20 1990	12:23	14° Ge 34' R
Jup	Retrograde	Nov 29 1990	21:18	13° Le 36' R
Mer	Retrograde	Dec 14 1990	14:02	10° Cp 00' R
Mar	Direct	Jan 1 1991	05:49	27° Ta 45' D
Mer	Direct	Jan 3 1991	10:45	23° Sg 43' D
Jup	Direct	Mar 30 1991	05:19	03° Le 33' D
Mer	Retrograde	Apr 4 1991	11:03	29° Ar 01' R
Mer	Direct	Apr 28 1991	02:44	18° Ar 00' D
Sat	Retrograde	May 16 1991	19:04	06° Aq 51' R
Ven	Retrograde	Aug 1 1991	03:33	07° Vi 19' R
Mer	Retrograde	Aug 7 1991	16:52	05° Vi 54' R
Mer	Direct	Aug 31 1991	07:28	23° Le 04' D
Ven	Direct	Sep 13 1991	01:53	21° Le 00' D
Sat	Direct	Oct 4 1991	19:08	00° Aq 12' D
Mer	Retrograde	Nov 28 1991	09:54	24° Sg 11' R
Mer	Direct	Dec 18 1991	04:05	07° Sg 56' D
Jup	Retrograde	Dec 30 1991	13:46	14° Vi 38' R
Mer	Retrograde	Mar 16 1992	17:27	11° Ar 18' R
Mer	Direct	Apr 8 1992	23:21	28° Pi 45' D
Jup	Direct	Apr 30 1992	11:46	04° Vi 38' D
Sat	Retrograde	May 28 1992	05:25	18° Aq 29' R
Mer	Retrograde	Jul 19 1992	17:48	17° Le 28' R
Mer	Direct	Aug 12 1992	19:47	05° Le 59' D
Sat	Direct	Oct 15 1992	18:03	11° Aq 49' D
Mer	Retrograde	Nov 11 1992	02:42	08° Sg 22' R
Mar	Retrograde	Nov 28 1992	16:23	27° Cn 37' R
Mer	Direct	Dec 1 1992	00:24	22° Sc 14' D
Jup	Retrograde	Jan 28 1993	15:36	14° Li 42' R
Mar	Direct	Feb 15 1993	00:38	08° Cn 41' D

Mer	Retrograde	Feb 27 1993	15:47	24° Pi 12' R
Ven	Retrograde	Mar 11 1993	02:26	20° Ar 01' R
Mer	Direct	Mar 22 1993	06:37	10° Pi 18' D
Ven	Direct	Apr 22 1993	07:09	03° Ar 45' D
Jup	Direct	May 31 1993	17:25	04° Li 45' D
Sat	Retrograde	Jun 9 1993	21:15	00° Pi 20' R
Mer	Retrograde	Jul 1 1993	08:22	28° Cn 15' R
Mer	Direct	Jul 25 1993	13:44	18° Cn 09' D
Mer	Retrograde	Oct 25 1993	15:33	22° Sc 30' R
Sat	Direct	Oct 27 1993	18:55	23° Aq 38' D
Mer	Direct	Nov 14 1993	22:32	06° Sc 33' D
Mer	Retrograde	Feb 11 1994	01:24	07° Pi 33' R
Jup	Retrograde	Feb 28 1994	06:24	14° Sc 39' R
Mer	Direct	Mar 4 1994	22:43	22° Aq 38' D
Mer	Retrograde	Jun 12 1994	10:43	08° Cn 25' R
Sat	Retrograde	Jun 22 1994	19:01	12° Pi 24' R
Jup	Direct	Jul 1 1994	19:49	04° Sc 46' D
Mer	Direct	Jul 6 1994	12:37	29° Ge 25' D
Mer	Retrograde	Oct 8 1994	23:37	06° Sc 28' R
Ven	Retrograde	Oct 12 1994	22:40	18° Sc 00' R
Mer	Direct	Oct 29 1994	20:58	20° Li 50' D
Sat	Direct	Nov 9 1994	00:22	05° Pi 41' D
Ven	Direct	Nov 23 1994	09:54	02° Sc 28' D
Mar	Retrograde	Jan 2 1995	14:19	02° Vi 40' R
Mer	Retrograde	Jan 25 1995	18:09	21° Aq 15' R
Mer	Direct	Feb 15 1995	22:00	05° Aq 38' D
Mar	Direct	Mar 24 1995	10:13	13° Le 10' D
Jup	Retrograde	Apr 1 1995	04:35	15° Sg 23' R
Mer	Retrograde	May 24 1995	01:58	18° Ge 21' R
Mer	Direct	Jun 16 1995	23:54	09° Ge 49' D
Sat	Retrograde	Jul 5 1995	23:38	24° Pi 45' R
Jup	Direct	Aug 2 1995	08:54	05° Sg 32' D
Mer	Retrograde	Sep 22 1995	02:09	20° Li 10' R
Mer	Direct	Oct 13 1995	17:41	05° Li 01' D
Sat	Direct	Nov 21 1995	11:41	18° Pi 00' D
Mer	Retrograde	Jan 9 1996	14:45	05° Aq 09' R
Mer	Direct	Jan 30 1996	03:10	19° Cp 08' D
Mer	Retrograde	May 3 1996	15:34	28° Ta 38' R
Jup	Retrograde	May 4 1996	07:52	17° Cp 39' R
Ven	Retrograde	May 19 1996	23:05	28° Ge 18' R
Mer	Direct	May 27 1996	11:56	19° Ta 39' D

Ven	Direct	Jul 1 1996	23:49	11° Ge 47' D
Sat	Retrograde	Jul 18 1996	12:23	07° Ar 24' R
Jup	Direct	Sep 3 1996	06:56	07° Cp 49' D
Mer	Retrograde	Sep 3 1996	22:41	03° Li 29' R
Mer	Direct	Sep 26 1996	10:02	19° Vi 00' D
Sat	Direct	Dec 3 1996	04:12	00° Ar 37' D
Mer	Retrograde	Dec 23 1996	12:39	19° Cp 13' R
Mer	Direct	Jan 12 1997	13:34	02° Cp 58' D
Mar	Retrograde	Feb 5 1997	17:28	05° Li 55' R
Mer	Retrograde	Apr 14 1997	16:56	09° Ta 39' R
Mar	Direct	Apr 27 1997	12:06	16° Vi 44' D
Mer	Direct	May 8 1997	11:01	29° Ar 29' D
Jup	Retrograde	Jun 9 1997	16:44	21° Aq 56' R
Sat	Retrograde	Aug 1 1997	08:32	20° Ar 22' R
Mer	Retrograde	Aug 17 1997	12:43	16° Vi 14' R
Mer	Direct	Sep 9 1997	18:36	02° Vi 43' D
Jup	Direct	Oct 7 1997	21:03	12° Aq 06' D
Mer	Retrograde	Dec 7 1997	09:49	03° Cp 22' R
Sat	Direct	Dec 16 1997	02:35	13° Ar 32' D
Ven	Retrograde	Dec 26 1997	14:17	03° Aq 56' R
Mer	Direct	Dec 27 1997	04:34	17° Sg 05' D
Ven	Direct	Feb 5 1998	14:24	18° Cp 28' D
Mer	Retrograde	Mar 27 1998	12:36	21° Ar 30' R
Mer	Direct	Apr 20 1998	00:25	09° Ar 48' D
Jup	Retrograde	Jul 17 1998	18:11	28° Pi 04' R
Mer	Retrograde	Jul 30 1998	19:23	28° Le 16' R
Sat	Retrograde	Aug 15 1998	10:48	03° Ta 38' R
Mer	Direct	Aug 23 1998	15:29	15° Le 58' D
Jup	Direct	Nov 13 1998	05:16	18° Pi 10' D
Mer	Retrograde	Nov 21 1998	04:39	17° Sg 32' R
Mer	Direct	Dec 10 1998	23:23	01° Sg 19' D
Sat	Direct	Dec 29 1998	07:44	26° Ar 46' D
Mer	Retrograde	Mar 10 1999	02:05	04° Ar 02' R
Mar	Retrograde	Mar 18 1999	06:41	12° Sc 12' R
Mer	Direct	Apr 2 1999	02:13	20° Pi 53' D
Mar	Direct	Jun 3 1999	23:06	24° Li 27' D
Mer	Retrograde	Jul 12 1999	16:26	09° Le 29' R
Ven	Retrograde	Jul 29 1999	18:39	05° Vi 08' R
Mer	Direct	Aug 5 1999	20:21	28° Cn 36' D
Jup	Retrograde	Aug 24 1999	19:01	04° Ta 59' R
Sat	Retrograde	Aug 29 1999	17:39	17° Ta 11' R

Ven	Direct	Sep 10 1999	17:20	18° Le 48' D
Mer	Retrograde	Nov 4 1999	19:53	01° Sg 43' R
Mer	Direct	Nov 24 1999	20:48	15° Sc 39' D
Jup	Direct	Dec 20 1999	07:24	25° Ar 01' D
Sat	Direct	Jan 11 2000	20:33	10° Ta 17' D
Mer	Retrograde	Feb 21 2000	05:40	17° Pi 10' R
Mer	Direct	Mar 14 2000	13:34	02° Pi 47' D
Mer	Retrograde	Jun 23 2000	01:28	19° Cn 57' R
Mer	Direct	Jul 17 2000	06:16	10° Cn 24' D
Sat	Retrograde	Sep 12 2000	03:44	00° Ge 59' R
Jup	Retrograde	Sep 29 2000	05:28	11° Ge 14' R
Mer	Retrograde	Oct 18 2000	06:34	15° Sc 47' R
Mer	Direct	Nov 7 2000	19:21	29° Li 58' D
Sat	Direct	Jan 24 2001	16:19	24° Ta 04' D
Jup	Direct	Jan 25 2001	01:02	01° Ge 11' D
Mer	Retrograde	Feb 3 2001	18:51	00° Pi 41' R
Mer	Direct	Feb 25 2001	08:35	15° Aq 25' D
Ven	Retrograde	Mar 8 2001	18:05	17° Ar 44' R
Ven	Direct	Apr 19 2001	21:30	01° Ar 28' D
Mar	Retrograde	May 11 2001	09:01	29° Sg 03' R
Mer	Retrograde	Jun 3 2001	22:16	29° Ge 58' R
Mer	Direct	Jun 27 2001	22:43	21° Ge 17' D
Mar	Direct	Jul 19 2001	15:45	15° Sg 07' D
Sat	Retrograde	Sep 26 2001	15:53	14° Ge 58' R
Mer	Retrograde	Oct 1 2001	12:17	29° Li 41' R
Mer	Direct	Oct 22 2001	17:16	14° Li 13' D
Jup	Retrograde	Nov 2 2001	07:54	15° Cn 41' R
Mer	Retrograde	Jan 18 2002	13:44	14° Aq 29' R
Sat	Direct	Feb 7 2002	17:41	08° Ge 02' D
Mer	Direct	Feb 8 2002	10:22	28° Cp 38' D
Jup	Direct	Mar 1 2002	07:18	05° Cn 37' D
Mer	Retrograde	May 15 2002	11:45	09° Ge 59' R
Mer	Direct	Jun 8 2002	08:07	01° Ge 22' D
Mer	Retrograde	Sep 14 2002	12:32	13° Li 15' R
Mer	Direct	Oct 6 2002	12:19	28° Vi 19' D
Ven	Retrograde	Oct 10 2002	11:33	15° Sc 36' R
Sat	Retrograde	Oct 11 2002	04:29	29° Ge 05' R
Ven	Direct	Nov 21 2002	00:11	00° Sc 04' D
Jup	Retrograde	Dec 4 2002	04:22	18° Le 06' R
Mer	Retrograde	Jan 2 2003	11:12	28° Cp 28' R
Mer	Direct	Jan 22 2003	18:02	12° Cp 18' D

Sat	Direct	Feb 21 2003	23:24	22° Ge 08' D
Jup	Direct	Apr 3 2003	19:14	08° Le 04' D
Mer	Retrograde	Apr 26 2003	04:54	20° Ta 32' R
Mer	Direct	May 20 2003	00:29	11° Ta 08' D
Mar	Retrograde	Jul 29 2003	00:33	10° Pi 08' R
Mer	Retrograde	Aug 28 2003	06:36	26° Vi 19' R
Mer	Direct	Sep 20 2003	01:46	12° Vi 13' D
Mar	Direct	Sep 27 2003	00:44	00° Pi 07' D
Sat	Retrograde	Oct 25 2003	15:38	13° Cn 14' R
Mer	Retrograde	Dec 17 2003	08:54	12° Cp 33' R
Jup	Retrograde	Jan 3 2004	16:05	18° Vi 54' R
Mer	Direct	Jan 6 2004	06:38	26° Sg 17' D
Sat	Direct	Mar 7 2004	08:08	06° Cn 17' D
Mer	Retrograde	Apr 6 2004	13:22	01° Ta 55' R
Mer	Direct	Apr 30 2004	05:59	21° Ar 07' D
Jup	Direct	May 4 2004	19:31	08° Vi 55' D
Ven	Retrograde	May 17 2004	15:25	26° Ge 08' R
Ven	Direct	Jun 29 2004	16:13	09° Ge 38' D
Mer	Retrograde	Aug 9 2004	17:27	08° Vi 46' R
Mer	Direct	Sep 2 2004	06:03	25° Le 45' D
Sat	Retrograde	Nov 7 2004	23:00	27° Cn 21' R
Mer	Retrograde	Nov 30 2004	05:10	26° Sg 44' R
Mer	Direct	Dec 19 2004	23:22	10° Sg 28' D
Jup	Retrograde	Feb 1 2005	18:46	18° Li 52' R
Mer	Retrograde	Mar 19 2005	17:09	14° Ar 05' R
Sat	Direct	Mar 21 2005	18:30	20° Cn 24' D
Mer	Direct	Apr 12 2005	00:40	01° Ar 45' D
Jup	Direct	Jun 4 2005	23:50	08° Li 56' D
Mer	Retrograde	Jul 22 2005	19:55	20° Le 28' R
Mer	Direct	Aug 15 2005	20:45	08° Le 46' D
Mar	Retrograde	Oct 1 2005	15:05	23° Ta 22' R
Mer	Retrograde	Nov 13 2005	22:36	10° Sg 55' R
Sat	Retrograde	Nov 22 2005	00:40	11° Le 19' R
Mer	Direct	Dec 3 2005	19:17	24° Sc 45' D
Mar	Direct	Dec 9 2005	20:56	08° Ta 14' D
Ven	Retrograde	Dec 24 2005	02:35	01° Aq 28' R
Ven	Direct	Feb 3 2006	02:14	16° Cp 02' D
Mer	Retrograde	Mar 2 2006	13:23	26° Pi 55' R
Jup	Retrograde	Mar 4 2006	10:21	18° Sc 52' R
Mer	Direct	Mar 25 2006	06:37	13° Pi 11' D
Sat	Direct	Apr 5 2006	04:54	04° Le 22' D

Mer	Retrograde	Jul 4 2006	12:28	01° Le 22' R
Jup	Direct	Jul 5 2006	23:43	08° Sc 59' D
Mer	Direct	Jul 28 2006	17:33	21° Cn 04' D
Mer	Retrograde	Oct 28 2006	12:09	25° Sc 05' R
Mer	Direct	Nov 17 2006	17:18	09° Sc 04' D
Sat	Retrograde	Dec 5 2006	19:12	25° Le 04' R
Mer	Retrograde	Feb 13 2007	21:31	10° Pi 12' R
Mer	Direct	Mar 7 2007	21:38	25° Aq 25' D
Jup	Retrograde	Apr 5 2007	17:44	19° Sg 47' R
Sat	Direct	Apr 19 2007	13:33	18° Le 09' D
Mer	Retrograde	Jun 15 2007	16:34	11° Cn 35' R
Mer	Direct	Jul 9 2007	19:10	02° Cn 29' D
Ven	Retrograde	Jul 27 2007	10:24	02° Vi 57' R
Jup	Direct	Aug 6 2007	18:38	09° Sg 56' D
Ven	Direct	Sep 8 2007	09:11	16° Le 35' D
Mer	Retrograde	Oct 11 2007	20:54	09° Sc 04' R
Mer	Direct	Nov 1 2007	15:52	23° Li 22' D
Mar	Retrograde	Nov 15 2007	01:16	12° Cn 27' R
Sat	Retrograde	Dec 19 2007	05:56	08° Vi 34' R
Mer	Retrograde	Jan 28 2008	13:25	23° Aq 52' R
Mar	Direct	Jan 30 2008	15:27	24° Ge 05' D
Mer	Direct	Feb 18 2008	19:51	08° Aq 20' D
Sat	Direct	May 2 2008	18:28	01° Vi 41' D
Jup	Retrograde	May 9 2008	04:14	22° Cp 22' R
Mer	Retrograde	May 26 2008	08:43	21° Ge 32' R
Mer	Direct	Jun 19 2008	07:27	12° Ge 59' D
Jup	Direct	Sep 7 2008	20:46	12° Cp 32' D
Mer	Retrograde	Sep 24 2008	00:11	22° Li 49' R
Mer	Direct	Oct 15 2008	12:59	07° Li 34' D
Sat	Retrograde	Dec 31 2008	09:54	21° Vi 46' R
Mer	Retrograde	Jan 11 2009	09:37	07° Aq 45' R
Mer	Direct	Feb 1 2009	00:04	21° Cp 46' D
Ven	Retrograde	Mar 6 2009	10:12	15° Ar 27' R
Ven	Direct	Apr 17 2009	12:21	29° Pi 12' D
Mer	Retrograde	May 6 2009	21:55	01° Ge 44' R
Sat	Direct	May 16 2009	17:44	14° Vi 55' D
Mer	Direct	May 30 2009	18:16	22° Ta 53' D
Jup	Retrograde	Jun 15 2009	00:19	27° Aq 01' R
Mer	Retrograde	Sep 6 2009	21:39	06° Li 12' R
Mer	Direct	Sep 29 2009	06:07	21° Vi 37' D
Jup	Direct	Oct 12 2009	20:54	17° Aq 10' D

Mar	Retrograde	Dec 20 2009	06:19	19° Le 42' R
Mer	Retrograde	Dec 26 2009	07:31	21° Cp 47' R
Sat	Retrograde	Jan 13 2010	07:14	04° Li 39' R
Mer	Direct	Jan 15 2010	09:46	05° Cp 34' D
Mar	Direct	Mar 10 2010	10:02	00° Le 18' D
Mer	Retrograde	Apr 17 2010	21:01	12° Ta 37' R
Mer	Direct	May 11 2010	15:21	02° Ta 40' D
Sat	Direct	May 30 2010	10:19	27° Vi 50' D
Jup	Retrograde	Jul 23 2010	04:13	03° Ar 24' R
Mer	Retrograde	Aug 20 2010	12:53	19° Vi 03' R
Mer	Direct	Sep 12 2010	16:02	05° Vi 23' D
Ven	Retrograde	Oct 8 2010	00:03	13° Sc 13' R
Jup	Direct	Nov 18 2010	09:11	23° Pi 30' D
Ven	Direct	Nov 18 2010	14:14	27° Li 39' D
Mer	Retrograde	Dec 10 2010	04:58	05° Cp 55' R
Mer	Direct	Dec 30 2010	00:14	19° Sg 39' D

Appendix II

These tables were calculated using Solar Fire for Windows, v. 4.12
© 1994-1998 Esoteric Technologies Pty. Ltd.
Time given is PDT (7 hours west of Greenwich)

Table 16 - Outer Planet Stations 1920-2010

Plu	Direct	Mar 19 1920	11:11	05° Cn 40' D
Nep	Direct	Apr 19 1920	02:06	08° Le 45' D
Ura	Retrograde	Jun 9 1920	18:55	05° Pi 40' R
Plu	Retrograde	Oct 9 1920	03:43	08° Cn 55' R
Ura	Direct	Nov 10 1920	21:43	01° Pi 45' D
Nep	Retrograde	Nov 15 1920	20:56	13° Le 46' R
Plu	Direct	Mar 20 1921	19:19	06° Cn 48' D
Nep	Direct	Apr 21 1921	14:04	10° Le 58' D
Ura	Retrograde	Jun 14 1921	01:35	09° Pi 38' R
Plu	Retrograde	Oct 10 1921	13:09	10° Cn 04' R
Ura	Direct	Nov 15 1921	03:17	05° Pi 43' D
Nep	Retrograde	Nov 18 1921	08:35	15° Le 58' R
Plu	Direct	Mar 22 1922	05:08	07° Cn 56' D
Nep	Direct	Apr 24 1922	02:49	13° Le 10' D
Ura	Retrograde	Jun 18 1922	10:32	13° Pi 36' R
Plu	Retrograde	Oct 12 1922	00:42	11° Cn 13' R
Ura	Direct	Nov 19 1922	08:59	09° Pi 41' D
Nep	Retrograde	Nov 20 1922	18:24	18° Le 11' R
Plu	Direct	Mar 23 1923	13:03	09° Cn 05' D
Nep	Direct	Apr 26 1923	13:59	15° Le 23' D
Ura	Retrograde	Jun 22 1923	17:20	17° Pi 33' R
Plu	Retrograde	Oct 13 1923	10:23	12° Cn 23' R
Nep	Retrograde	Nov 23 1923	05:17	20° Le 23' R
Ura	Direct	Nov 23 1923	14:04	13° Pi 38' D
Plu	Direct	Mar 23 1924	23:07	10° Cn 14' D
Nep	Direct	Apr 28 1924	03:16	17° Le 35' D
Ura	Retrograde	Jun 26 1924	02:30	21° Pi 31' R
Plu	Retrograde	Oct 13 1924	22:10	13° Cn 34' R
Nep	Retrograde	Nov 24 1924	15:39	22° Le 36' R
Ura	Direct	Nov 26 1924	19:13	17° Pi 36' D
Plu	Direct	Mar 25 1925	08:02	11° Cn 24' D
Nep	Direct	Apr 30 1925	14:12	19° Le 48' D
Ura	Retrograde	Jun 30 1925	09:49	25° Pi 28' R

Plu	Retrograde	Oct 15 1925	09:40	14° Cn 45' R	
Nep	Retrograde	Nov 27 1925	01:38	24° Le 48' R	
Ura	Direct	Dec 1 1925	00:04	21° Pi 33' D	
Plu	Direct	Mar 26 1926	17:12	12° Cn 35' D	
Nep	Direct	May 3 1926	03:11	22° Le 00' D	
Ura	Retrograde	Jul 4 1926	19:06	29° Pi 26' R	
Plu	Retrograde	Oct 16 1926	21:00	15° Cn 57' R	
Nep	Retrograde	Nov 29 1926	12:41	27° Le 00' R	
Ura	Direct	Dec 5 1926	05:04	25° Pi 31' D	
Plu	Direct	Mar 28 1927	03:40	13° Cn 47' D	
Nep	Direct	May 5 1927	14:01	24° Le 11' D	
Ura	Retrograde	Jul 9 1927	02:45	03° Ar 25' R	
Plu	Retrograde	Oct 18 1927	10:27	17° Cn 09' R	
Nep	Retrograde	Dec 1 1927	22:10	29° Le 11' R	
Ura	Direct	Dec 9 1927	09:59	29° Pi 30' D	
Plu	Direct	Mar 28 1928	12:15	14° Cn 59' D	
Nep	Direct	May 7 1928	02:12	26° Le 23' D	
Ura	Retrograde	Jul 12 1928	12:15	07° Ar 24' R	
Plu	Retrograde	Oct 18 1928	22:20	18° Cn 23' R	
Nep	Retrograde	Dec 3 1928	09:58	01° Vi 23' R	
Ura	Direct	Dec 12 1928	15:15	03° Ar 28' D	
Plu	Direct	Mar 29 1929	23:24	16° Cn 12' D	
Nep	Direct	May 9 1929	13:38	28° Le 35' D	
Ura	Retrograde	Jul 16 1929	20:01	11° Ar 23' R	
Plu	Retrograde	Oct 20 1929	12:25	19° Cn 38' R	
Nep	Retrograde	Dec 5 1929	19:32	03° Vi 35' R	
Ura	Direct	Dec 16 1929	20:22	07° Ar 27' D	
Plu	Direct	Mar 31 1930	09:25	17° Cn 26' D	
Nep	Direct	May 12 1930	01:04	00° Vi 47' D	
Ura	Retrograde	Jul 21 1930	05:33	15° Ar 23' R	
Plu	Retrograde	Oct 22 1930	01:30	20° Cn 53' R	
Nep	Retrograde	Dec 8 1930	07:06	05° Vi 47' R	
Ura	Direct	Dec 21 1930	01:43	11° Ar 27' D	
Plu	Direct	Apr 1 1931	20:18	18° Cn 41' D	
Nep	Direct	May 14 1931	13:14	03° Vi 00' D	
Ura	Retrograde	Jul 25 1931	13:39	19° Ar 23' R	
Plu	Retrograde	Oct 23 1931	15:12	22° Cn 10' R	
Nep	Retrograde	Dec 10 1931	17:02	07° Vi 59' R	
Ura	Direct	Dec 25 1931	07:06	15° Ar 26' D	

Plu	Direct	Apr 2 1932	08:24	19° Cn 57' D
Nep	Direct	May 16 1932	00:12	05° Vi 12' D
Ura	Retrograde	Jul 28 1932	23:32	23° Ar 24' R
Plu	Retrograde	Oct 24 1932	05:52	23° Cn 27' R
Nep	Retrograde	Dec 12 1932	03:43	10° Vi 11' R
Ura	Direct	Dec 28 1932	12:30	19° Ar 27' D
Plu	Direct	Apr 3 1933	19:19	21° Cn 14' D
Nep	Direct	May 18 1933	13:21	07° Vi 24' D
Ura	Retrograde	Aug 2 1933	08:30	27° Ar 25' R
Plu	Retrograde	Oct 25 1933	19:07	24° Cn 46' R
Nep	Retrograde	Dec 14 1933	14:12	12° Vi 23' R
Ura	Direct	Jan 1 1934	18:08	23° Ar 28' D
Plu	Direct	Apr 5 1934	08:40	22° Cn 32' D
Nep	Direct	May 21 1934	00:15	09° Vi 36' D
Ura	Retrograde	Aug 6 1934	18:59	01° Ta 27' R
Plu	Retrograde	Oct 27 1934	10:49	26° Cn 05' R
Nep	Retrograde	Dec 16 1934	23:49	14° Vi 35' R
Ura	Direct	Jan 5 1935	23:49	27° Ar 30' D
Plu	Direct	Apr 6 1935	20:21	23° Cn 50' D
Nep	Direct	May 23 1935	13:28	11° Vi 48' D
Ura	Retrograde	Aug 11 1935	05:03	05° Ta 31' R
Plu	Retrograde	Oct 29 1935	01:03	27° Cn 25' R
Nep	Retrograde	Dec 19 1935	10:33	16° Vi 47' R
Ura	Direct	Jan 10 1936	05:51	01° Ta 33' D
Plu	Direct	Apr 7 1936	09:31	25° Cn 09' D
Nep	Direct	May 25 1936	00:34	13° Vi 59' D
Ura	Retrograde	Aug 14 1936	16:37	09° Ta 35' R
Plu	Retrograde	Oct 29 1936	16:59	28° Cn 46' R
Nep	Retrograde	Dec 20 1936	19:27	18° Vi 58' R
Ura	Direct	Jan 13 1937	12:09	05° Ta 37' D
Plu	Direct	Apr 8 1937	23:02	26° Cn 30' D
Nep	Direct	May 27 1937	13:14	16° Vi 11' D
Ura	Retrograde	Aug 19 1937	03:58	13° Ta 41' R
Plu	Retrograde	Oct 31 1937	09:12	00° Le 08' R
Nep	Retrograde	Dec 23 1937	06:26	21° Vi 09' R
Ura	Direct	Jan 17 1938	19:01	09° Ta 43' D
Plu	Direct	Apr 10 1938	11:37	27° Cn 51' D
Nep	Direct	May 30 1938	01:00	18° Vi 22' D
Ura	Retrograde	Aug 23 1938	16:35	17° Ta 49' R
Plu	Retrograde	Nov 2 1938	01:15	01° Le 31' R

Nep	Retrograde	Dec 25 1938	15:19	23° Vi 20' R
Ura	Direct	Jan 22 1939	02:08	13° Ta 50' D
Plu	Direct	Apr 12 1939	02:18	29° Cn 13' D
Nep	Direct	Jun 1 1939	12:32	20° Vi 33' D
Ura	Retrograde	Aug 28 1939	05:22	21° Ta 58' R
Plu	Retrograde	Nov 3 1939	19:43	02° Le 55' R
Nep	Retrograde	Dec 28 1939	02:11	25° Vi 31' R
Ura	Direct	Jan 26 1940	10:22	17° Ta 59' D
Plu	Direct	Apr 12 1940	15:23	00° Le 37' D
Nep	Direct	Jun 3 1940	00:44	22° Vi 44' D
Ura	Retrograde	Aug 31 1940	18:52	26° Ta 09' R
Plu	Retrograde	Nov 4 1940	12:32	04° Le 20' R
Nep	Retrograde	Dec 29 1940	11:46	27° Vi 42' R
Ura	Direct	Jan 29 1941	18:45	22° Ta 09' D
Plu	Direct	Apr 14 1941	06:38	02° Le 02' D
Nep	Direct	Jun 5 1941	11:19	24° Vi 54' D
Ura	Retrograde	Sep 5 1941	08:55	00° Ge 21' R
Plu	Retrograde	Nov 6 1941	07:58	05° Le 47' R
Nep	Retrograde	Dec 31 1941	22:16	29° Vi 53' R
Ura	Direct	Feb 3 1942	04:34	26° Ta 21' D
Plu	Direct	Apr 15 1942	21:28	03° Le 28' D
Nep	Direct	Jun 7 1942	23:52	27° Vi 06' D
Ura	Retrograde	Sep 9 1942	23:00	04° Ge 35' R
Plu	Retrograde	Nov 8 1942	02:33	07° Le 15' R
Nep	Retrograde	Jan 3 1943	08:56	02° Li 04' R
Ura	Direct	Feb 7 1943	14:25	00° Ge 34' D
Plu	Direct	Apr 17 1943	12:50	04° Le 55' D
Nep	Direct	Jun 10 1943	10:16	29° Vi 17' D
Ura	Retrograde	Sep 14 1943	14:07	08° Ge 51' R
Plu	Retrograde	Nov 9 1943	21:51	08° Le 45' R
Nep	Retrograde	Jan 5 1944	18:34	04° Li 15' R
Ura	Direct	Feb 12 1944	01:44	04° Ge 50' D
Plu	Direct	Apr 18 1944	06:05	06° Le 24' D
Nep	Direct	Jun 11 1944	23:04	01° Li 28' D
Ura	Retrograde	Sep 18 1944	05:01	13° Ge 08' R
Plu	Retrograde	Nov 10 1944	18:20	10° Le 16' R
Nep	Retrograde	Jan 7 1945	05:47	06° Li 26' R
Ura	Direct	Feb 15 1945	12:52	09° Ge 06' D
Plu	Direct	Apr 19 1945	22:00	07° Le 54' D
Nep	Direct	Jun 14 1945	09:56	03° Li 39' D

Ura	Retrograde	Sep 22 1945	21:22	17° Ge 27' R	
Plu	Retrograde	Nov 12 1945	13:38	11° Le 48' R	
Nep	Retrograde	Jan 9 1946	14:52	08° Li 37' R	
Ura	Direct	Feb 20 1946	01:44	13° Ge 25' D	
Plu	Direct	Apr 21 1946	16:39	09° Le 26' D	
Nep	Direct	Jun 16 1946	22:30	05° Li 50' D	
Ura	Retrograde	Sep 27 1946	13:10	21° Ge 48' R	
Plu	Retrograde	Nov 14 1946	11:38	13° Le 22' R	
Nep	Retrograde	Jan 12 1947	02:04	10° Li 48' R	
Ura	Direct	Feb 24 1947	14:01	17° Ge 45' D	
Plu	Direct	Apr 23 1947	09:59	10° Le 59' D	
Nep	Direct	Jun 19 1947	10:15	08° Li 02' D	
Ura	Retrograde	Oct 2 1947	07:03	26° Ge 10' R	
Plu	Retrograde	Nov 16 1947	08:03	14° Le 57' R	
Nep	Retrograde	Jan 14 1948	11:06	13° Li 00' R	
Ura	Direct	Feb 29 1948	04:32	22° Ge 07' D	
Plu	Direct	Apr 24 1948	04:58	12° Le 33' D	
Nep	Direct	Jun 20 1948	22:12	10° Li 13' D	
Ura	Retrograde	Oct 5 1948	23:56	00° Cn 35' R	
Plu	Retrograde	Nov 17 1948	06:39	16° Le 34' R	
Nep	Retrograde	Jan 15 1949	21:35	15° Li 11' R	
Ura	Direct	Mar 4 1949	18:07	26° Ge 30' D	
Plu	Direct	Apr 26 1949	00:25	14° Le 09' D	
Nep	Direct	Jun 23 1949	10:52	12° Li 24' D	
Ura	Retrograde	Oct 10 1949	19:29	05° Cn 01' R	
Plu	Retrograde	Nov 19 1949	05:16	18° Le 12' R	
Nep	Retrograde	Jan 18 1950	07:02	17° Li 21' R	
Ura	Direct	Mar 9 1950	10:17	00° Cn 56' D	
Plu	Direct	Apr 27 1950	19:13	15° Le 46' D	
Nep	Direct	Jun 25 1950	21:52	14° Li 35' D	
Ura	Retrograde	Oct 15 1950	13:40	09° Cn 29' R	
Plu	Retrograde	Nov 21 1950	04:29	19° Le 52' R	
Nep	Retrograde	Jan 20 1951	16:49	19° Li 32' R	
Ura	Direct	Mar 14 1951	01:22	05° Cn 24' D	
Plu	Direct	Apr 29 1951	16:30	17° Le 25' D	
Nep	Direct	Jun 28 1951	10:52	16° Li 45' D	
Ura	Retrograde	Oct 20 1951	10:47	14° Cn 00' R	
Plu	Retrograde	Nov 23 1951	05:32	21° Le 33' R	
Nep	Retrograde	Jan 23 1952	03:07	21° Li 43' R	
Ura	Direct	Mar 17 1952	19:20	09° Cn 54' D	

Plu	Direct	Apr 30 1952	12:00	19° Le 05' D
Nep	Direct	Jun 29 1952	21:26	18° Li 56' D
Ura	Retrograde	Oct 24 1952	06:22	18° Cn 32' R
Plu	Retrograde	Nov 24 1952	05:43	23° Le 16' R
Nep	Retrograde	Jan 24 1953	12:25	23° Li 53' R
Ura	Direct	Mar 22 1953	12:13	14° Cn 26' D
Plu	Direct	May 2 1953	10:11	20° Le 48' D
Nep	Direct	Jul 2 1953	10:08	21° Li 06' D
Ura	Retrograde	Oct 29 1953	04:43	23° Cn 06' R
Plu	Retrograde	Nov 26 1953	08:46	25° Le 01' R
Nep	Retrograde	Jan 26 1954	23:36	26° Li 04' R
Ura	Direct	Mar 27 1954	08:24	19° Cn 00' D
Plu	Direct	May 4 1954	07:46	22° Le 32' D
Nep	Direct	Jul 4 1954	20:38	23° Li 17' D
Ura	Retrograde	Nov 3 1954	01:19	27° Cn 42' R
Plu	Retrograde	Nov 28 1954	10:31	26° Le 48' R
Nep	Retrograde	Jan 29 1955	08:46	28° Li 14' R
Ura	Direct	Apr 1 1955	03:12	23° Cn 36' D
Plu	Direct	May 6 1955	06:35	24° Le 18' D
Nep	Direct	Jul 7 1955	08:37	25° Li 28' D
Ura	Retrograde	Nov 8 1955	00:31	02° Le 20' R
Plu	Retrograde	Nov 30 1955	14:32	28° Le 37' R
Nep	Retrograde	Jan 31 1956	20:17	00° Sc 25' R
Ura	Direct	Apr 5 1956	01:26	28° Cn 13' D
Plu	Direct	May 7 1956	06:58	26° Le 06' D
Nep	Direct	Jul 8 1956	20:00	27° Li 39' D
Ura	Retrograde	Nov 11 1956	21:53	06° Le 59' R
Plu	Retrograde	Dec 1 1956	18:08	00° Vi 27' R
Nep	Retrograde	Feb 2 1957	05:45	02° Sc 36' R
Ura	Direct	Apr 9 1957	22:13	02° Le 52' D
Plu	Direct	May 9 1957	06:40	27° Le 55' D
Nep	Direct	Jul 11 1957	07:36	29° Li 50' D
Ura	Retrograde	Nov 16 1957	21:33	11° Le 40' R
Plu	Retrograde	Dec 3 1957	22:35	02° Vi 20' R
Nep	Retrograde	Feb 4 1958	16:40	04° Sc 47' R
Ura	Direct	Apr 14 1958	22:00	07° Le 32' D
Plu	Direct	May 11 1958	09:16	29° Le 47' D
Nep	Direct	Jul 13 1958	19:53	02° Sc 00' D
Ura	Retrograde	Nov 21 1958	19:46	16° Le 22' R
Plu	Retrograde	Dec 6 1958	04:28	04° Vi 14' R

Nep	Retrograde	Feb 7 1959	02:41	06° Sc 58' R
Ura	Direct	Apr 19 1959	20:31	12° Le 13' D
Plu	Direct	May 13 1959	10:29	01° Vi 40' D
Nep	Direct	Jul 16 1959	06:54	04° Sc 11' D
Ura	Retrograde	Nov 26 1959	19:35	21° Le 05' R
Plu	Retrograde	Dec 8 1959	09:27	06° Vi 10' R
Nep	Retrograde	Feb 9 1960	12:36	09° Sc 08' R
Ura	Direct	Apr 23 1960	21:27	16° Le 56' D
Plu	Direct	May 14 1960	14:25	03° Vi 35' D
Nep	Direct	Jul 17 1960	20:02	06° Sc 22' D
Ura	Retrograde	Nov 30 1960	18:44	25° Le 48' R
Plu	Retrograde	Dec 9 1960	17:17	08° Vi 08' R
Nep	Retrograde	Feb 10 1961	23:18	11° Sc 19' R
Ura	Direct	Apr 28 1961	21:35	21° Le 39' D
Plu	Direct	May 16 1961	17:42	05° Vi 32' D
Nep	Direct	Jul 20 1961	06:55	08° Sc 33' D
Ura	Retrograde	Dec 5 1961	18:41	00° Vi 33' R
Plu	Retrograde	Dec 11 1961	23:44	10° Vi 08' R
Nep	Retrograde	Feb 13 1962	08:22	13° Sc 29' R
Ura	Direct	May 3 1962	23:20	26° Le 24' D
Plu	Direct	May 18 1962	22:18	07° Vi 31' D
Nep	Direct	Jul 22 1962	20:05	10° Sc 43' D
Ura	Retrograde	Dec 10 1962	18:43	05° Vi 18' R
Plu	Retrograde	Dec 14 1962	09:09	12° Vi 10' R
Nep	Retrograde	Feb 15 1963	19:17	15° Sc 40' R
Ura	Direct	May 9 1963	00:45	01° Vi 09' D
Plu	Direct	May 21 1963	03:55	09° Vi 32' D
Nep	Direct	Jul 25 1963	06:57	12° Sc 53' D
Ura	Retrograde	Dec 15 1963	18:52	10° Vi 04' R
Plu	Retrograde	Dec 16 1963	18:01	14° Vi 14' R
Nep	Retrograde	Feb 18 1964	04:12	17° Sc 50' R
Ura	Direct	May 13 1964	02:56	05° Vi 55' D
Plu	Direct	May 22 1964	09:05	11° Vi 35' D
Nep	Direct	Jul 26 1964	19:19	15° Sc 04' D
Plu	Retrograde	Dec 18 1964	04:37	16° Vi 20' R
Ura	Retrograde	Dec 19 1964	19:46	14° Vi 51' R
Nep	Retrograde	Feb 19 1965	15:27	20° Sc 00' R
Ura	Direct	May 18 1965	05:49	10° Vi 42' D
Plu	Direct	May 24 1965	16:54	13° Vi 41' D
Nep	Direct	Jul 29 1965	06:41	17° Sc 14' D

Plu	Retrograde	Dec 20 1965	16:06	18° Vi 28' R
Ura	Retrograde	Dec 24 1965	19:52	19° Vi 38' R
Nep	Retrograde	Feb 22 1966	01:02	22° Sc 11' R
Ura	Direct	May 23 1966	08:18	15° Vi 29' D
Plu	Direct	May 26 1966	23:18	15° Vi 48' D
Nep	Direct	Jul 31 1966	17:52	19° Sc 24' D
Plu	Retrograde	Dec 23 1966	03:47	20° Vi 39' R
Ura	Retrograde	Dec 29 1966	21:17	24° Vi 26' R
Nep	Retrograde	Feb 24 1967	12:00	24° Sc 21' R
Ura	Direct	May 28 1967	12:32	20° Vi 17' D
Plu	Direct	May 29 1967	09:07	17° Vi 58' D
Nep	Direct	Aug 3 1967	05:47	21° Sc 35' D
Plu	Retrograde	Dec 25 1967	17:28	22° Vi 52' R
Ura	Retrograde	Jan 3 1968	20:50	29° Vi 13' R
Nep	Retrograde	Feb 26 1968	22:28	26° Sc 32' R
Plu	Direct	May 30 1968	18:00	20° Vi 10' D
Ura	Direct	Jun 1 1968	15:25	25° Vi 04' D
Nep	Direct	Aug 4 1968	16:16	23° Sc 46' D
Plu	Retrograde	Dec 27 1968	06:03	25° Vi 07' R
Ura	Retrograde	Jan 7 1969	22:13	04° Li 00' R
Nep	Retrograde	Feb 28 1969	08:56	28° Sc 43' R
Plu	Direct	Jun 2 1969	05:16	22° Vi 24' D
Ura	Direct	Jun 6 1969	20:36	29° Vi 52' D
Nep	Direct	Aug 7 1969	04:49	25° Sc 56' D
Plu	Retrograde	Dec 29 1969	21:20	27° Vi 24' R
Ura	Retrograde	Jan 12 1970	21:07	08° Li 48' R
Nep	Retrograde	Mar 2 1970	20:23	00° Sg 53' R
Plu	Direct	Jun 4 1970	16:53	24° Vi 41' D
Ura	Direct	Jun 11 1970	23:40	04° Li 39' D
Nep	Direct	Aug 9 1970	15:15	28° Sc 07' D
Plu	Retrograde	Jan 1 1971	11:04	29° Vi 42' R
Ura	Retrograde	Jan 17 1971	21:50	13° Li 34' R
Nep	Retrograde	Mar 5 1971	06:02	03° Sg 04' R
Plu	Direct	Jun 7 1971	05:12	26° Vi 59' D
Ura	Direct	Jun 17 1971	05:02	09° Li 26' D
Nep	Direct	Aug 12 1971	04:02	00° Sg 18' D
Plu	Retrograde	Jan 4 1972	03:35	02° Li 03' R
Ura	Retrograde	Jan 22 1972	19:58	18° Li 19' R
Nep	Retrograde	Mar 6 1972	17:48	05° Sg 15' R
Plu	Direct	Jun 8 1972	19:33	29° Vi 19' D

Ura	Direct	Jun 21 1972	08:01	14° Li 12' D
Nep	Direct	Aug 13 1972	14:54	02° Sg 29' D
Plu	Retrograde	Jan 5 1973	18:54	04° Li 26' R
Ura	Retrograde	Jan 26 1973	19:46	23° Li 04' R
Nep	Retrograde	Mar 9 1973	03:15	07° Sg 26' R
Plu	Direct	Jun 11 1973	09:05	01° Li 40' D
Ura	Direct	Jun 26 1973	13:04	18° Li 56' D
Nep	Direct	Aug 16 1973	03:24	04° Sg 40' D
Plu	Retrograde	Jan 8 1974	12:05	06° Li 50' R
Ura	Retrograde	Jan 31 1974	17:00	27° Li 47' R
Nep	Retrograde	Mar 11 1974	14:46	09° Sg 37' R
Plu	Direct	Jun 14 1974	01:20	04° Li 04' D
Ura	Direct	Jul 1 1974	15:34	23° Li 40' D
Nep	Direct	Aug 18 1974	14:59	06° Sg 51' D
Plu	Retrograde	Jan 11 1975	05:19	09° Li 15' R
Ura	Retrograde	Feb 5 1975	15:43	02° Sc 28' R
Nep	Retrograde	Mar 14 1975	00:31	11° Sg 48' R
Plu	Direct	Jun 16 1975	16:00	06° Li 29' D
Ura	Direct	Jul 6 1975	19:27	28° Li 21' D
Nep	Direct	Aug 21 1975	02:40	09° Sg 01' D
Plu	Retrograde	Jan 13 1976	23:06	11° Li 43' R
Ura	Retrograde	Feb 10 1976	12:10	07° Sc 09' R
Nep	Retrograde	Mar 15 1976	11:18	13° Sg 58' R
Plu	Direct	Jun 18 1976	09:43	08° Li 56' D
Ura	Direct	Jul 10 1976	21:20	03° Sc 02' D
Nep	Direct	Aug 22 1976	14:58	11° Sg 12' D
Plu	Retrograde	Jan 15 1977	18:28	14° Li 11' R
Ura	Retrograde	Feb 14 1977	09:53	11° Sc 47' R
Nep	Retrograde	Mar 17 1977	22:01	16° Sg 09' R
Plu	Direct	Jun 21 1977	01:59	11° Li 24' D
Ura	Direct	Jul 15 1977	23:32	07° Sc 41' D
Nep	Direct	Aug 25 1977	01:30	13° Sg 22' D
Plu	Retrograde	Jan 18 1978	13:04	16° Li 42' R
Ura	Retrograde	Feb 19 1978	05:52	16° Sc 24' R
Nep	Retrograde	Mar 20 1978	08:27	18° Sg 19' R
Plu	Direct	Jun 23 1978	20:40	13° Li 54' D
Ura	Direct	Jul 21 1978	00:39	12° Sc 19' D
Nep	Direct	Aug 27 1978	13:56	15° Sg 33' D
Plu	Retrograde	Jan 21 1979	09:50	19° Li 13' R
Ura	Retrograde	Feb 24 1979	02:16	21° Sc 00' R

Nep	Retrograde	Mar 22 1979	20:14	20° Sg 30' R
Plu	Direct	Jun 26 1979	14:48	16° Li 25' D
Ura	Direct	Jul 26 1979	01:06	16° Sc 55' D
Nep	Direct	Aug 30 1979	00:01	17° Sg 43' D
Plu	Retrograde	Jan 24 1980	04:58	21° Li 46' R
Ura	Retrograde	Feb 28 1980	21:38	25° Sc 34' R
Nep	Retrograde	Mar 24 1980	06:26	22° Sg 41' R
Plu	Direct	Jun 28 1980	10:24	18° Li 58' D
Ura	Direct	Jul 30 1980	01:31	21° Sc 30' D
Nep	Direct	Aug 31 1980	12:25	19° Sg 54' D
Plu	Retrograde	Jan 26 1981	02:32	24° Li 21' R
Ura	Retrograde	Mar 4 1981	16:41	00° Sg 07' R
Nep	Retrograde	Mar 26 1981	18:54	24° Sg 51' R
Plu	Direct	Jul 1 1981	06:53	21° Li 32' D
Ura	Direct	Aug 4 1981	00:28	26° Sc 03' D
Nep	Direct	Sep 2 1981	22:50	22° Sg 05' D
Plu	Retrograde	Jan 28 1982	22:09	26° Li 56' R
Ura	Retrograde	Mar 9 1982	11:06	04° Sg 38' R
Nep	Retrograde	Mar 29 1982	05:10	27° Sg 03' R
Plu	Direct	Jul 4 1982	03:11	24° Li 07' D
Ura	Direct	Aug 8 1982	23:55	00° Sg 35' D
Nep	Direct	Sep 5 1982	10:41	24° Sg 16' D
Plu	Retrograde	Jan 31 1983	19:49	29° Li 32' R
Ura	Retrograde	Mar 14 1983	04:32	09° Sg 07' R
Nep	Retrograde	Mar 31 1983	17:38	29° Sg 14' R
Plu	Direct	Jul 7 1983	01:28	26° Li 43' D
Ura	Direct	Aug 13 1983	21:09	05° Sg 04' D
Nep	Direct	Sep 7 1983	22:00	26° Sg 28' D
Plu	Retrograde	Feb 3 1984	15:39	02° Sc 08' R
Ura	Retrograde	Mar 17 1984	21:47	13° Sg 34' R
Nep	Retrograde	Apr 2 1984	04:23	01° Cp 25' R
Plu	Direct	Jul 8 1984	22:21	29° Li 19' D
Ura	Direct	Aug 17 1984	19:36	09° Sg 32' D
Nep	Direct	Sep 9 1984	09:33	28° Sg 39' D
Plu	Retrograde	Feb 5 1985	12:45	04° Sc 45' R
Ura	Retrograde	Mar 22 1985	13:29	17° Sg 59' R
Nep	Retrograde	Apr 4 1985	16:04	03° Cp 37' R
Plu	Direct	Jul 11 1985	21:44	01° Sc 55' D
Ura	Direct	Aug 22 1985	15:04	13° Sg 58' D
Nep	Direct	Sep 11 1985	21:51	00° Cp 51' D

Plu	Retrograde	Feb 8 1986	09:00	07° Sc 22' R
Ura	Retrograde	Mar 27 1986	05:28	22° Sg 22' R
Nep	Retrograde	Apr 7 1986	03:24	05° Cp 49' R
Plu	Direct	Jul 14 1986	19:03	04° Sc 32' D
Ura	Direct	Aug 27 1986	12:00	18° Sg 21' D
Nep	Direct	Sep 14 1986	08:45	03° Cp 02' D
Plu	Retrograde	Feb 11 1987	05:15	09° Sc 58' R
Ura	Retrograde	Mar 31 1987	19:15	26° Sg 44' R
Nep	Retrograde	Apr 9 1987	14:03	08° Cp 00' R
Plu	Direct	Jul 17 1987	18:48	07° Sc 09' D
Ura	Direct	Sep 1 1987	05:35	22° Sg 43' D
Nep	Direct	Sep 16 1987	21:38	05° Cp 14' D
Plu	Retrograde	Feb 14 1988	02:01	12° Sc 35' R
Ura	Retrograde	Apr 4 1988	10:03	01° Cp 03' R
Nep	Retrograde	Apr 11 1988	02:09	10° Cp 12' R
Plu	Direct	Jul 19 1988	16:18	09° Sc 45' D
Ura	Direct	Sep 5 1988	00:37	27° Sg 03' D
Nep	Direct	Sep 18 1988	08:13	07° Cp 25' D
Plu	Retrograde	Feb 15 1989	21:34	15° Sc 11' R
Ura	Retrograde	Apr 8 1989	22:36	05° Cp 20' R
Nep	Retrograde	Apr 13 1989	12:24	12° Cp 23' R
Plu	Direct	Jul 22 1989	15:44	12° Sc 22' D
Ura	Direct	Sep 9 1989	16:14	01° Cp 20' D
Nep	Direct	Sep 20 1989	20:57	09° Cp 37' D
Plu	Retrograde	Feb 18 1990	18:33	17° Sc 47' R
Ura	Retrograde	Apr 13 1990	12:25	09° Cp 35' R
Nep	Retrograde	Apr 16 1990	00:55	14° Cp 34' R
Plu	Direct	Jul 25 1990	13:14	14° Sc 58' D
Ura	Direct	Sep 14 1990	09:02	05° Cp 36' D
Nep	Direct	Sep 23 1990	07:20	11° Cp 48' D
Plu	Retrograde	Feb 21 1991	13:23	20° Sc 23' R
Ura	Retrograde	Apr 17 1991	23:56	13° Cp 49' R
Nep	Retrograde	Apr 18 1991	11:28	16° Cp 46' R
Plu	Direct	Jul 28 1991	12:00	17° Sc 34' D
Ura	Direct	Sep 18 1991	22:44	09° Cp 50' D
Nep	Direct	Sep 25 1991	19:09	13° Cp 59' D
Plu	Retrograde	Feb 24 1992	10:03	22° Sc 57' R
Nep	Retrograde	Apr 20 1992	00:18	18° Cp 57' R
Ura	Retrograde	Apr 21 1992	13:06	18° Cp 01' R
Plu	Direct	Jul 30 1992	10:07	20° Sc 09' D

Ura	Direct	Sep 22 1992	13:48	14° Cp 03' D
Nep	Direct	Sep 27 1992	06:14	16° Cp 11' D
Plu	Retrograde	Feb 26 1993	04:09	25° Sc 31' R
Nep	Retrograde	Apr 22 1993	11:41	21° Cp 09' R
Ura	Retrograde	Apr 25 1993	23:43	22° Cp 11' R
Plu	Direct	Aug 2 1993	08:06	22° Sc 43' D
Ura	Direct	Sep 27 1993	01:53	18° Cp 14' D
Nep	Direct	Sep 29 1993	17:13	18° Cp 23' D
Plu	Retrograde	Feb 28 1994	23:47	28° Sc 04' R
Nep	Retrograde	Apr 25 1994	00:04	23° Cp 21' R
Ura	Retrograde	Apr 30 1994	12:11	26° Cp 21' R
Plu	Direct	Aug 5 1994	06:30	25° Sc 17' D
Ura	Direct	Oct 1 1994	15:17	22° Cp 23' D
Nep	Direct	Oct 2 1994	05:07	20° Cp 34' D
Plu	Retrograde	Mar 3 1995	16:51	00° Sg 36' R
Nep	Retrograde	Apr 27 1995	12:15	25° Cp 33' R
Ura	Retrograde	May 4 1995	21:49	00° Aq 28' R
Plu	Direct	Aug 8 1995	03:27	27° Sc 49' D
Nep	Direct	Oct 4 1995	15:34	22° Cp 46' D
Ura	Direct	Oct 6 1995	02:10	26° Cp 32' D
Plu	Retrograde	Mar 5 1996	10:46	03° Sg 07' R
Nep	Retrograde	Apr 29 1996	00:03	27° Cp 45' R
Ura	Retrograde	May 8 1996	09:32	04° Aq 35' R
Plu	Direct	Aug 10 1996	01:52	00° Sg 20' D
Nep	Direct	Oct 6 1996	04:09	24° Cp 59' D
Ura	Direct	Oct 9 1996	14:09	00° Aq 38' D
Plu	Retrograde	Mar 8 1997	03:09	05° Sg 36' R
Nep	Retrograde	May 1 1997	13:09	29° Cp 57' R
Ura	Retrograde	May 12 1997	18:22	08° Aq 40' R
Plu	Direct	Aug 12 1997	21:53	02° Sg 50' D
Nep	Direct	Oct 8 1997	14:43	27° Cp 11' D
Ura	Direct	Oct 14 1997	00:00	04° Aq 44' D
Plu	Retrograde	Mar 10 1998	18:54	08° Sg 04' R
Nep	Retrograde	May 4 1998	00:06	02° Aq 10' R
Ura	Retrograde	May 17 1998	05:00	12° Aq 45' R
Plu	Direct	Aug 15 1998	19:34	05° Sg 18' D
Nep	Direct	Oct 11 1998	03:31	29° Cp 23' D
Ura	Direct	Oct 18 1998	10:40	08° Aq 49' D
Plu	Retrograde	Mar 13 1999	10:31	10° Sg 30' R
Nep	Retrograde	May 6 1999	13:13	04° Aq 22' R

Ura	Retrograde	May 21 1999	12:49	16° Aq 48' R
Plu	Direct	Aug 18 1999	14:18	07° Sg 44' D
Nep	Direct	Oct 13 1999	14:26	01° Aq 35' D
Ura	Direct	Oct 22 1999	19:27	12° Aq 52' D
Plu	Retrograde	Mar 15 2000	00:08	12° Sg 54' R
Nep	Retrograde	May 7 2000	23:57	06° Aq 34' R
Ura	Retrograde	May 24 2000	22:36	20° Aq 49' R
Plu	Direct	Aug 20 2000	10:28	10° Sg 09' D
Nep	Direct	Oct 15 2000	02:44	03° Aq 47' D
Ura	Direct	Oct 26 2000	04:53	16° Aq 54' D
Plu	Retrograde	Mar 17 2001	15:07	15° Sg 17' R
Nep	Retrograde	May 10 2001	12:55	08° Aq 47' R
Ura	Retrograde	May 29 2001	05:36	24° Aq 50' R
Plu	Direct	Aug 23 2001	03:54	12° Sg 32' D
Nep	Direct	Oct 17 2001	14:06	06° Aq 00' D
Ura	Direct	Oct 30 2001	12:24	20° Aq 55' D
Plu	Retrograde	Mar 20 2002	03:38	17° Sg 38' R
Nep	Retrograde	May 13 2002	00:19	10° Aq 59' R
Ura	Retrograde	Jun 2 2002	14:50	28° Aq 50' R
Plu	Direct	Aug 25 2002	21:53	14° Sg 54' D
Nep	Direct	Oct 20 2002	01:19	08° Aq 12' D
Ura	Direct	Nov 3 2002	20:20	24° Aq 54' D
Plu	Retrograde	Mar 22 2003	17:17	19° Sg 57' R
Nep	Retrograde	May 15 2003	12:47	13° Aq 11' R
Ura	Retrograde	Jun 6 2003	21:28	02° Pi 49' R
Plu	Direct	Aug 28 2003	14:29	17° Sg 14' D
Nep	Direct	Oct 22 2003	13:15	10° Aq 24' D
Ura	Direct	Nov 8 2003	02:45	28° Aq 54' D
Plu	Retrograde	Mar 24 2004	04:16	22° Sg 15' R
Nep	Retrograde	May 17 2004	01:19	15° Aq 24' R
Ura	Retrograde	Jun 10 2004	06:37	06° Pi 48' R
Plu	Direct	Aug 30 2004	06:58	19° Sg 32' D
Nep	Direct	Oct 23 2004	23:28	12° Aq 36' D
Ura	Direct	Nov 11 2004	09:26	02° Pi 52' D
Plu	Retrograde	Mar 26 2005	16:52	24° Sg 31' R
Nep	Retrograde	May 19 2005	13:29	17° Aq 36' R
Ura	Retrograde	Jun 14 2005	13:24	10° Pi 46' R
Plu	Direct	Sep 1 2005	22:31	21° Sg 49' D
Nep	Direct	Oct 26 2005	11:42	14° Aq 49' D
Ura	Direct	Nov 15 2005	14:55	06° Pi 51' D

Plu	Retrograde	Mar 29 2006	03:02	26° Sg 45' R	
Nep	Retrograde	May 22 2006	03:02	19° Aq 49' R	
Ura	Retrograde	Jun 18 2006	22:27	14° Pi 44' R	
Plu	Direct	Sep 4 2006	12:44	24° Sg 05' D	
Nep	Direct	Oct 28 2006	21:41	17° Aq 02' D	
Ura	Direct	Nov 19 2006	20:46	10° Pi 49' D	
Plu	Retrograde	Mar 31 2007	13:18	28° Sg 58' R	
Nep	Retrograde	May 24 2007	14:54	22° Aq 02' R	
Ura	Retrograde	Jun 23 2007	05:24	18° Pi 42' R	
Plu	Direct	Sep 7 2007	03:55	26° Sg 18' D	
Nep	Direct	Oct 31 2007	09:59	19° Aq 15' D	
Ura	Direct	Nov 24 2007	01:40	14° Pi 46' D	
Plu	Retrograde	Apr 1 2008	22:55	01° Cp 09' R	
Nep	Retrograde	May 26 2008	05:01	24° Aq 15' R	
Ura	Retrograde	Jun 26 2008	14:43	22° Pi 39' R	
Plu	Direct	Sep 8 2008	16:27	28° Sg 30' D	
Nep	Direct	Nov 1 2008	20:32	21° Aq 28' D	
Ura	Direct	Nov 27 2008	07:10	18° Pi 44' D	
Plu	Retrograde	Apr 4 2009	06:42	03° Cp 18' R	
Nep	Retrograde	May 28 2009	16:47	26° Aq 29' R	
Ura	Retrograde	Jun 30 2009	21:49	26° Pi 37' R	
Plu	Direct	Sep 11 2009	06:16	00° Cp 39' D	
Nep	Direct	Nov 4 2009	08:24	23° Aq 41' D	
Ura	Direct	Dec 1 2009	11:52	22° Pi 42' D	
Plu	Retrograde	Apr 6 2010	14:58	05° Cp 25' R	
Nep	Retrograde	May 31 2010	06:46	28° Aq 42' R	
Ura	Retrograde	Jul 5 2010	07:12	00° Ar 35' R	
Plu	Direct	Sep 13 2010	17:55	02° Cp 47' D	
Nep	Direct	Nov 6 2010	19:55	25° Aq 55' D	
Ura	Direct	Dec 5 2010	17:17	26° Pi 40' D	

Appendix III
Lecture, Class & Workshop Tapes by the Author

UAC 2002 Conference Orlando **"Introduction to Progression Theory"** Lecture $9.95

UAC 2002 Conference Orlando **"Pragmatic Guidance for the Self-Employed Astrologer"** Lecture $9.95

South Florida Astrological Association 2002 **"The Spiritual Dimension of the Ascendant"** Lecture $9.95

ISAR 2000 **"Progression Theory & Transit Triggers"** Lecture $9.95

ISAR 2000 **"Secondary, Tertiary & Minor Progressed Client Counseling"** Lecture $9.95

Astrological Conference of Western Canada 1997 **"The Ascendant"** Lecture $9.95

Astrological Conference of Western Canada 1996 **"Secondary Progressions"** Lecture $9.95

UAC '95 Conference Monterey **"Multiple Levels of the Outer Planets"** Lecture $9.95

Vision '94 Conference San Diego **"Solar System Model of Planetary Consciousness"** Lecture $9.95

Vision '94 Conference San Diego **"Partners Who Activate Our Shadow"** Lecture $9.95

South Florida Astrological Association 2002 **"Mundane Astrology"** Workshop (3 tapes) $16.95
Cardinal ingress charts; Jupiter-Saturn conjunctions; geodetic methods; eclipses; Saros cycles, 9/11

South Florida Astrological Association 2002 **"The Astrology of Relationship"** Workshop (3 tapes) $16.95
How to prepare for a relationship analysis consultation (synastry & composite); case history

Astrological Association of St. Petersburg 2002 **"Multi-Dim. of Progressions"** Workshop (3 tapes) $16.95
Secondary, Tertiary & Minor inter-relationship with natal & transits; lunations; retrogradation; stations

Ast Research Guild of Orlando 2001 **"Partners Who Activate Our Shadow"** Workshop (3 tapes) $16.95
Karmic relationship theory; relationship as transformation; Chiron and healing dimensions of love

Earthwalk School of Astrology 1999 **"Esoteric Astrology"** Workshop (2 tapes) $16.95
Spiritual meanings of the different levels of planetary intelligence revealed to us through their glyphs

Earthwalk School of Astrology 1999 **"Sabian Aspect Orbs"** Workshop (2 tapes) $16.95
Sabian Symbols define angular separation between planets; waxing, waning, applying and separating

Earthwalk School of Astrology 1999 **"Sabian Symbols"** Workshop (2 tapes) $16.95
Origin and history; significant natal degrees; meaningful current progressed degrees

Earthwalk School of Astrology 1999 **"Medical Astrology"** Workshop (2 tapes) $16.95
Constitutional analysis; body-mind connection; planetary weakness; Yods; hard natal aspects

Earthwalk School of Astrology 1998 **"Neptune in Aquarius (1998-2012)"** Workshop (2 tapes) $16.95
Previous Neptune in Aquarius periods (1506-1520, 1670-1684, 1834-1848); plus generational effect

Earthwalk School of Astrology 1998 **"The Ascendant"** Workshop (2 tapes) $16.95
12 versions of each rising sign; chart ruler; prog. ascendant; transits to the ascendant; Sabian symbols

Earthwalk School of Astrology 1998 **"Karmic Astrology"** Workshop (2 tapes) $16.95
Nodes; retrograde planets; twelfth house; interceptions; eclipses; ascendant; the Moon; Saturn; Pluto

Earthwalk School of Astrology 1998 **"Jupiter & Saturn"** Workshop (2 tapes) $16.95
Realms of social and spiritual involvement; by sign, house, aspect, house rulership, transit and prog.

Earthwalk School of Astrology 1998 **"Transforming Loss to Gain"** Workshop (2 tapes) $16.95
Pluto; Scorpio; 8th house; loss, death and renewal in life; emotionally ravaged soul coming back to life

Earthwalk School of Astrology 1998 **"The Lunar Nodes"** Workshop (2 tapes) $16.95
Patterns from past lives; soul purpose; transiting nodes; nodes in synastry and composite charts

Earthwalk School of Astrology 1998 **"Electional Astrology"** Workshop (2 tapes) $16.95
Techniques for picking a wedding date; scheduling medical surgery; starting a business & more

Astrological Conference of Western Canada 1997 **"Astrology & Anger"** Workshop (2 tapes) $16.95
Examines the four patterns of anger as defined by the stressful aspects to Mars, Saturn, Uranus & Pluto

Astrology: A Language of Life • **Complete Set of Eight Two-Hour Beginning Class Tapes $89.95**
Week 1: Elements, Modes & Zodiac Signs • Week 2: Planets • Week 3: Houses • Week 4: Aspects I
Week 5: Aspects II • Week 6: Patterns & Configurations • Week 7: Chart Synthesis • Week 8: Examples

Chart Interpretation Handbook by Stephen Arroyo • Beginning Class Textbook $12.95

see next page for ordering instructions

Intermediate Astrology Class • **Complete Set of Eight Two-Hour Class Tapes $109.95**
Week 1: Retrogrades • Week 2: Transits • Week 3: Progressions • Week 4: Lunar Nodes & Life Purpose
Week 5: Relationship Analysis Techniques • Week 6: Aspects & 360° Cycle Analysis
Week 7: Solar Returns • Week 8: House Rulerships, Interceptions & Dispositors

Class Tapes Include Handouts, Reading Assignments, Written Essays & Recommended Book List

To Order by Mail or Phone:

Add $1.00 postage per lecture; $2.00 per workshop; or $7.50 per class up to maximum $10 postage
Earthwalk School of Astrology PO Box 620679 Woodside CA 94062 USA 1.800.778.8490
ewastro@earthlink.net • MasterCard/VISA accepted • e-mail for a postage quotation abroad

Appendix IV
Astrology Software Programs

For Windows

Solar Fire 5: The Complete Professional Calculation Program	call for current price
ACS PC Atlas: American & International	call for current price
Order Solar Fire 5 & PC Atlas together—1/2 off of Atlas price	call for current price
Solar Maps: Relocation Interpretations; Eclipse Paths	call for current price
JigSaw 2: Rectification; Research; Family Patterns	call for current price
Kepler 6.0: The Complete Professional Calculation Program	call for current price
Kepler Report Options: Dozens of Report Writers in Many Languages	call for current price

For Macintosh

Io Edition: The Complete Professional Calculation Program	call for current price
Star*Sprite: Time Machine; Research; Event Searching; Color Charts	call for current price
Io Detective: Search Chart Files For Like Criteria (signs, houses, aspects)	call for current price
Io Atlas: American & International Atlas For Macintosh	call for current price
Io Series Interpreters: Io Horoscope (natal); Io Forecast (transits); Io Relationship (synastry & composite)	call for current price
Specially Priced Packages: Multiple Programs @ Substantial Savings	call for current price

To Order Programs or Request Catalogues:

call or write

**Earthwalk School of Astrology
PO Box 620679
Woodside CA 94062 USA
1.800.778.8490
ewastro@earthlink.net**

MasterCard/VISA accepted

Appendix V
Computer Chart Services

Natal Chart + Data Page
Yearly Progressed Hit List
Monthly Transit Search (Sun thru Mars)
90° or 360° Midpoint Sort
Natal/Transit Bi-Wheel
Lunar Return (Standard or Precessed)
Synastry Table (Interchart Aspects)
Composite Chart

Yearly Transit Search (Mars thru Pluto)
Progressed Chart
6-Month Graphic Ephemeris
Natal/Progressed/Transit Tri-Wheel
Solar Return (Standard or Precessed)
End of Life Chart
Time-Space Relationship Chart
Lifetime Secondary Lunations

1 or 2 charts ordered - $5.00 ea. • 3 or more charts ordered - $4.00 ea. + $1.00 postage/order

Lifetime Tertiary Lunations   Lifetime Minor Lunations

$10.00 ea. + $1.00 postage

Complete Natal Chart Sabian Aspect Orb Summary
(Includes every angular separation between all planets along with the corresponding Sabian Symbols)

$25.00 + $1.00 postage

Specify Options

House Division System: Placidus   Koch   Equal   Porphyry   Campanus   Natural
Planets/Chiron/Asteroids: Planets Only   Planets & Chiron   Planets, Asteroids & Chiron
Aspect Lines: Ptolemaic Only (Conjunction, Sextile, Square, Trine, Opposition)
Add Quincunxes; Add Semi-Squares; Add Sesquiquadrates; No Aspect Lines (Hub Chart)
Chartwheel Style: American (houses equally sized)   European (houses shown in actual size)
Lunar Nodes: True Node   Mean Node
Other Options: Add Part of Fortune   Add Node Aspects   Add ASC & MC Aspects

To Order Charts:

call or write

Earthwalk School of Astrology
PO Box 620679
Woodside CA 94062 USA
1.800.778.8490
ewastro@earthlink.net

MasterCard/VISA accepted

Appendix VI
Contacting the Author

To Write the Author

Correspondence may be sent to:

Earthwalk School of Astrology
PO Box 620679
Woodside CA 94062 USA

ewastro@earthlink.net

Author Availability for Lectures/Workshops

Mr. Blaschke is available to lecture and teach workshops on Progressions and many other astrological techniques and topics.

To request lecture/workshop synopses for your local astrological association, conference faculty or symposium, please write the publisher.

Author Availability for Telephone Consultation

Mr. Blaschke is available for personal consultation over the telephone. One-hour progression analysis appointments can be scheduled through the publisher. Call 1.800.778.8490 for appointment scheduling.

Bibliography

Astrology, Psychology & The Four Elements • Stephen Arroyo • CRCS • 1975

Astrology, Karma & Transformation • Stephen Arroyo • CRCS • 1978

Relationships & Life Cycles • Stephen Arroyo • CRCS • 1979

The Rulership Book • Rex E. Bills • Macoy Publishing • 1971

Astrology: A Language of Life; Volume II - Sabian Aspect Orbs
Robert P. Blaschke • Earthwalk School of Astrology • 2000

An Encyclopædia of Psychological Astrology • Charles E.O. Carter • L.N. Fowler & Co. • 1924

The Principles of Astrology • Charles E.O. Carter • L.N. Fowler & Co. • 1925

The Seven Great Problems of Astrology • Charles E.O. Carter • L.N. Fowler & Co. • 1927

The Zodiac and the Soul • Charles E.O. Carter • L.N. Fowler & Co. • 1928

Symbolic Directions in Modern Astrology • Charles E.O. Carter • L.N. Fowler & Co. • 1929

The Astrological Aspects • Charles E.O. Carter • L.N. Fowler & Co. • 1930

The Astrology of Accidents • Charles E.O. Carter • L.N. Fowler & Co. • 1932

Some Principles of Horoscopic Delineation • Charles E.O. Carter • L.N. Fowler & Co. • 1934

Essays on the Foundations of Astrology • Charles E.O. Carter • L.N. Fowler & Co. • 1947

An Introduction to Political Astrology • Charles E.O. Carter • L.N. Fowler & Co. • 1951

The Degrees of the Zodiac Symbolised • Charubel • L.N. Fowler & Co. • 1898

Encyclopedia Of Astrology • Nicholas deVore • Philosophical Library • 1957

Pluto: The Evolutionary Journey of the Soul • Jeff Green • Llewellyn • 1985

The Outer Planets & Their Cycles • Liz Greene • CRCS • 1983

Planets In Transit • Robert Hand • Whitford Press • 1976

Secondary Progressions • Nancy Hastings • Samuel Weiser • 1984

The Sabian Symbols in Astrology • Marc Edmund Jones • Aurora Press • 1993

The Progressed Horoscope • Alan Leo • L.N. Fowler & Co. Ltd. • 1906

Esoteric Astrology • Alan Leo • L.N. Fowler & Co. Ltd. • 1967

Mars: the War Lord • Alan Leo • Samuel Weiser • 1970

Jupiter: the Preserver • Alan Leo • Samuel Weiser • 1970

Saturn: the Reaper • Alan Leo • Samuel Weiser • 1970

The Astrology of Self-Discovery • Tracy Marks • CRCS • 1985

The Art Of Chart Interpretation • Tracy Marks • CRCS • 1986

The Astrologer's Astronomical Handbook • Jeff Mayo • L.N. Fowler & Co. Ltd. • 1965

The Solar Return Book of Prediction • Raymond A. Merriman • Seek-It Publishing • 1977

Astrology, The Divine Science • Marcia Moore & Mark Douglas • Arcane • 1971

Modern Transits • Lois M. Rodden • AFA • 1978

An Astrological Mandala: The Cycle of Transformations and Its 360 Symbolic Phases
Dane Rudhyar • Random House • 1973

Cycles of Becoming • Alexander Ruperti • CRCS • 1978

Karmic Astrology, Volume I: The Moon's Nodes and Reincarnation
Martin Schulman • Samuel Weiser • 1975

Karmic Astrology, Volume II: Retrogrades & Reincarnation
Martin Schulman • Samuel Weiser • 1977

Dynamics Of Aspect Analysis • Bil Tierney • CRCS • 1983

The Sacred Heart of Astrology Correspondence Course

A Two-Year Correspondence Course Designed to Transform
the Student into a Self-Employed Professional Astrologer

Taught by Robert P. Blaschke of Earthwalk School of Astrology

Internationally respected and trusted as a full-time
professional consulting, lecturing & teaching astrologer

Business Skills ~ Personal Support ~ Practical Guidance

As Uranus enters the sign of the Fishes: a Christ-Centered approach to astrology.

You can study astrology forever, but an intention to love and serve clients
will transform your heart and make you into a professional astrologer.

Module I - Client Preparation
Lesson I-I: A Christ-centered approach to client work
Lesson I-II: Preparing for your natal consultation
Lesson I-III: Preparing for your progressed & transit consultation
Lesson I-IV: Preparing for your solar return consultation
Lesson I-V: Preparing for your relationship analysis consultation
Lesson I-VI: Preparing for your electional consultation

Module II - Advanced Technique
Lesson II-I: Retrograde planets, the Lunar Nodes & Karmic astrology
Lesson II-II: The Midheaven & Vocational astrology
Lesson II-III: Medical astrology
Lesson II-IV: Esoteric astrology & Sabian Aspect Orbs
Lesson II-V: Multi-Dimensional Progressions
Lesson II-VI: Chart Rectification

Module III - Astrological Self-Employment
Lesson III-I: Creating your multi-faceted astrology business plan
Lesson III-II: Establishing your professional practice
Lesson III-III: Handling income, expenses & taxes
Lesson III-IV: Marketing & advertising
Lesson III-V: Navigating the client relationship
Lesson III-VI: Overcoming occupational hazards & fostering personal growth

Module IV - Establishing Yourself as a Professional
Lesson IV-I: Teaching astrology & local public speaking
Lesson IV-II: Researching & writing astrological articles
Lesson IV-III: Writing your first book
Lesson IV-IV: Starting your publishing company
Lesson IV-V: Joining the lecture circuit & earning income on the road
Lesson IV-VI: Participating in local and national astrological organizations

Four six-month modules ~ Twenty-four lessons in all ~ One taped lesson a month
Self-paced ~ Subsequent lessons are sent only after completion of prior lesson

Tuition: $2,400⁺

MasterCard or VISA accepted

⁺10% discount for pre-payment in full.
Tuition payable in four $600 payments; one due at the start of each module.

www.earthwalkastrology.com